KUNDALIN

Om Swami is a mystic who lives in the Himalayan foothills. An advanced yogi, Swami has done thousands of hours of intense meditation in complete seclusion in Himalayan caves and woods.

Prior to renunciation, he founded and ran a multi-million-dollar software company with offices in San Francisco, New York, Toronto, London, Sydney and India.

Swami is also the author of the best-selling *If Truth be Told: A Monk's Memoir* and *The Wellness Sense*. You can connect with him on his blog, omswami.com, which is read by millions all over the world.

KUNDALINI — AN UNTOLD STORY

A Himalayan Mystic's Insight into the Power of
Kundalini and Chakra *Sadhana*

OM SWAMI

Published in India by Jaico Publishing House

Worldwide publishing rights: Black Lotus Press

Copyright © Om Swami 2016

P-ISBN: 978-0-9940027-9-2
E-ISBN: 978-0-9940027-2-3

Om Swami asserts the moral right to be identified
as the author of this work.

www.omswami.com

|| Om Śrī mātrai namaḥ ||

Dedicated to the Divine in You

Prātarūt'thāya sāyāhnaṁ sāyāhanāt prātarēva tu,
Yatkrōmi jaganmātastadēva tava pūjanam.

From the moment I wake up at dawn till dusk, and from dusk till dawn, O Mother Divine, everything I do is an act of your worship.

CONTENTS

WHY THIS BOOK?

A lady visited me at the ashram. She was a mind-therapist and a healer (whatever that means) by profession, and was well acquainted with the concept of chakras. She believed in *vastu*, feng shui, and tarot. These were, in fact, the tools of her trade, so to speak. She was a little worried that day because a famous 'chakra expert' told her that the spin of her chakras was not right and it was affecting her work.

"Come again," I said, "what's not right about your chakras?"

"The spin," she replied, "the spin of my chakras is not right."

"What are you?" I chuckled, "a motor car that has gone out of spin?"

Not sure if I was serious or joking, she smiled a bit uncomfortably. I wasn't kidding, even though I laughed quietly for a few seconds. In fact, I felt sorry for her, like I do for all those seekers who are misguided by the 'chakra experts'.

"So, what else did he tell you?" I asked.

"He asked me to wear a chakra pendant and light special incense."

"Right, and what happens then?"

"It'll balance my chakras," and she pulled out a pendant. It looked pretty expensive. On beautiful four lotus petals made from white gold, there was a solitaire in the middle and the petals were studded with emerald, ruby, opal and topaz. "It's supposed to touch my heart," she said.

"It's touching your heart alright, but it's not doing much for the rest of you, now is it?"

All expression disappeared from her face but her lips that curled slightly downwards.

"Why is that so, Swami? I have spent so much money on this thing."

"Veena," I said, "this is a load of rubbish."

She looked downcast, and angry, as if someone had handed her a crystal for the price of a diamond.

"But I thought chakras were real."

"Of course chakras are real, Veena!"

"Then?"

"I meant that this whole business of balancing the chakras and all that gobbledygook are simply tricks to fool people. The only way to awaken the kundalini is by meditating over a prolonged period, that's all."

"So this chakra pendant won't make it faster for me?"

"If you can make nine ladies pregnant and deliver the baby in a month," I said, "then I suppose you could quickly awaken your kundalini too."

"Is it possible, Swami?" she asked me, most seriously.

I burst out laughing. It's amazing what all we are willing to believe, I thought.

Veena's is not an isolated case. I meet scores of gullible seekers all the time who want quick solutions. I'm amused when people walk into a nicely done up place, where there is this amorous kind of dim lighting, a small but expensive and antique-looking idol of Buddha or Shiva sits in a corner elegantly illuminated by the flame of a tea light. An oil burner is slowly diffusing scent in the air, nice music is playing in the background, plush couches, mahogany furniture, and they ask me, "Oh, do you feel the energy in this place, Swami?" I generally smile and let go of it, but which energy are they talking about, I haven't got the foggiest idea.

Yes, you feel nice, you feel good, but it's got nothing to do with chakras or energies. It's just the ambience. Personally, you'd be better off spending your time in a nice Ayurvedic spa, where at least you get the value for money, where they treat you and serve you as a customer and not milk you like a poor, ignorant, mislaid cow that has accidentally stepped into someone else's farm.

Chakra bracelets, pendants, incense, mats, rugs, clothes, wall hangings, chakra music, chakra programming and other attractive paraphernalia have absolutely no connection with the real *sadhana* of chakras. Anyone who claims to awaken your kundalini by touching you on your forehead (or wherever) is lying to you, no matter how genuine and charismatic that person might sound or appear.

Then there are those people who claim to see or read your chakras. They too are taking you for a ride. Seeing anyone's chakras has nothing to do with clairvoyance. There's nothing to see or read when it comes to chakras. Your chakras are not some chapters from a book that someone could just read. People talk about opening or closing chakras as if they were a jar of cookies with a lid that you could remove any time or put back on. The feeling of a snake-like sensation moving up your spine is not the awakening of the kundalini. If it persists, please check with a neurologist instead!

You may have heard how each chakra has a certain number of petals and different letters, various presiding deities, many attendant deities, different shapes and so on. Let me tell you, these are unnecessary complications. Understanding the real truth of chakras is a completely different ballgame.

"na rūpam asyeha tathopalabhyate
nānto na cādir na ca sampratiṣṭhā
aśvattham enaṁ su-virūḍha-mūlam
asaṅga-śastreṇa dṛḍhena chittvā

tataḥ padaṁ tat parimārgitavyaṁ
yasmin gatā na nivartanti bhūyaḥ
tam eva cādyaṁ puruṣaṁ prapadye
yataḥ pravṛttiḥ prasṛtā purāṇī"

(*Bhagavad Gita*, 15.3,4)

Krishna says to Arjuna, "Upon attainment one finds that the truth is not what it had been made out to be. The real form of the tree of life is imperceptible; it has neither beginning nor end. The one, who cuts it from the roots with great detachment, reaches an irreversible state of tranquility. He reaches a shore from where there is no return. He returns to his source."

This is also the truth of the kundalini, the reality of the chakras. Whatever you may have seen, heard or read about it so far is not the truth, at least not the complete truth. The day you actually experience the piercing of the chakras or awakening of the kundalini, you will reach an irreversible state of bliss, a point of no return.

Milk once churned into butter cannot transform back to being milk again. Similarly, once you discover your true nature, no matter what happens, your old tendencies, your negative emotions leave you completely. A selfless concern for the welfare of all sentient beings arises in you naturally. You grow out of your own shoes. It's not that you won't feel the pain if someone were to hit you. Of course, you will feel the pain. But, unlike your older self, the transformed you won't get angry at the one who is hurting you.

Awakening of the kundalini is reaching your innermost state of bliss and joy. This state is covered with ten layers – desire, anger, greed, attachment, ego, passion, jealousy, hatred, fear and self-concern. As you elevate spiritually, you start shedding these layers. These *avarana,* layers, veil the true you. The real you that is beyond the duality of pain and grief, good and bad, moral and immoral. Awakening is a steady and gradual process on the path of kundalini *sadhana.* It is not an instant realization. It builds up, it grows on you. With each level of awakening, you discover bit more about the new you and you shed bit more of the old you.

The science of the kundalini is an ancient *vidya* that has been passed through an oral tradition in strict disciplic succession to worthy recipients. The science remains just as intact today. All it requires is for one to walk the path with great determination and tenacity.

Let me take you to the source, for what is found in the roots can never be understood from the leaves. Let the boughs not baffle you. Let the fruits not distract you. You just have to nurture the roots and the whole tree will belong to you.

THE ORIGIN OF KUNDALINI
MEDITATION

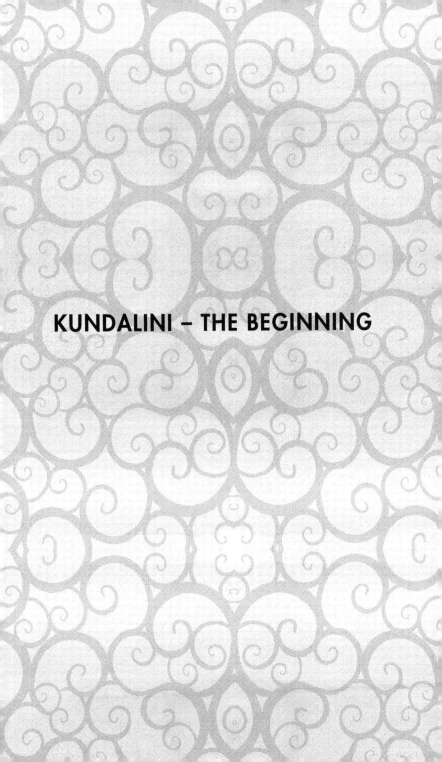

KUNDALINI – THE BEGINNING

Long before you and I existed in our current forms, earth was a beautiful place with abundance of forests, rich flora and fauna, and thousands of rivers and lakes. Some 900 million light years away in the interstellar space, a parallel universe existed with an earth-like planet, five times bigger and far more beautiful.

The sun in the solar system of this earth-like planet was twice the size of our sun. The days were longer, so were the nights. Giant predators roamed freely in its forests that were vaster than our oceans. The Himalayas, eight times the size of our Himalayas, were covered in snow. On those Himalayas, the biggest, widest and highest mountain summit was called Kailasha.

Kailasha is where Shiva, the eternal yogi, meditated and lived with his consort Sati. No one knows how Shiva was born. Some seers said he was born at the time of creation, out of lightning and thunder, while some said he had come from yet another universe and taken up his abode at Kailasha. It was with his yogic prowess that Shiva remained ever youthful, most charismatic and enchanting.

Once, Sati's father, the famed king Daksha, had organized one of the grandest and greatest *yajnas* ever known to anyone in three epochs. Brahma, Vishnu, Indra, *vasus*, *adityas* and numerous other *devas* were invited to this most exclusive *yajna*. The *ritwik* was none other than the great Brihaspati himself, overseeing every aspect, from the correct pronunciation of mantras to the offering of right oblations in the one hundred thousand fire pits built there.

The whole atmosphere was echoing with the sounds of conchs and most rhythmic Sanskrit chants, which were more invigorating than the nectar of Dhanavantri, the divine physician, and more heady than the wine served in *Indraloka*. Mammoth structures with utmost luxury had been erected to provide every comfort to the guests.

The place of *yajna* itself was a grand palace next to none and was a mix of open and enclosed areas. On wide pathways, numerous chariots, pulled by snow-white or jet-black steeds, were organized so invitees could move around. It was said that by our current measure of time it would take one seven days just to get from the first fire pit to the last one.

While all the *devas* were exulting in divine ecstasy at Daksha's palace, Shiva meditated quietly on Kailasha. This did not sit well with Sati.

"Should we not be at my father's *yajna*, my lord?" asked Sati, a little hesitatingly because she knew well that Shiva fathomed everything.

"No Sati," Shiva murmured in his deep voice like the Ganges flowing from his matted locks, "an honourable man must never go anywhere uninvited."

"But, it's my father, lord," she spoke softly. "He must have forgotten to invite us."

"Your father does not like Shiva, O innocent one," Shiva spoke lovingly, "because Shiva is sovereign and unbound by any custom."

"Please, can we go?" Sati tried her luck. "It's been ages since I last met my family."

"You can if you want, Sati. Shiva will not." Thus, he closed his eyes and plunged into *dhyana*.

Unable to resist the temptation, Sati, clad in the finest silk and adorned with the most precious jewels, called upon Shiva's *ganas*, who immediately arranged for a flying chariot.

From several miles away, Sati could smell the fragrance in the air. She could hear the chants, and the sound of conchs, vina and mridanga. She was already missing Shiva but she knew that Shiva only did what he had to do. As she got closer to the venue, she couldn't help but appreciate its magnanimity. It was unlike anything she had ever seen before.

As Sati descended from her chariot, hundreds of handmaids ran towards her; their very own Sati who was their princess at one time. They garlanded her with exquisite flowers that never withered. They spread petals of rose and lotuses on the path where she would walk. Some fanned her with handfans made from the feathers of Himalayan swans, some offered her betel nut, some sprinkled scent in the air. Giant conchs were blasted; *gandharvas* sang the welcome songs as she made way.

Sati walked around in search of her mother and sisters and saw that most glorious seats had been wrought for the *devas* and their consorts. With great eagerness and curiosity she went around looking for Shiva's seat but there was none. Sati's heart sank.

"Could this just be an oversight?" she thought. She felt relieved that Shiva was not there because his fury would have destroyed everything in a split second.

Meanwhile, queen Prasuti saw her daughter Sati and ran towards her. Out of her 24 daughters, she loved Sati the most because she knew that Sati was none other than the incarnation of Adya Shakti herself. Daksha stopped Prasuti midway and prohibited her from greeting Sati. Sati was taken aback by her father's demeanor, yet she proceeded to touch his feet. But, he withdrew.

The music suddenly stopped and everyone around looked at Daksha's stern face as he stood cross-armed with legs slightly apart. Both he and Sati were silent for a few moments. Realizing that her father was not going to speak first, she said:

"Where should I sit, father? I don't see Shiva's seat or mine next to his."

"Seat for that mendicant?" Daksha scoffed, "this is a royal gathering and not a feast for beggars and ascetics."

"Father!" Sati raised her voice.

"How could you even think that I'll invite an *aghori* like Shiva here?" Daksha continued with the tirade. "I disowned you the day you married that naked, ash-smeared eccentric. Only a pauper like him would send his wife uninvited."

"Father!" Sati cried, "Shiva is the lord of the lords."

"My foot," Daksha screamed, "with his rusty trident, he's not even fit to be a guard of my stable. He's only good for those decapitated, deformed, enslaved ghosts and residents of cremation grounds."

Sati cupped her jeweled ears with her pink and delicate hands. Her moonlike fair face turned crimson and tears began trickling down ceaselessly. Like a true *pativrata*, there was only one man Sati had ever loved and he was Shiva. An incarnate of Adya Shakti, the Supreme Energy herself, Sati well knew that Shiva was the God of the three worlds, an immortal yogi who was beyond destruction and mortality. Overcome with a great sense of guilt for hearing such terrible things about Shiva, she felt she had violated her *pativrata* dharma.

In that instant Sati realized why the omniscient Shiva had forbidden her from attending the *yajna*. Recalling her conversation with Shiva, she repented for not listening to him. She felt that by hurting Shiva, she no longer deserved to live.

"Daksha!" Sati's eyes turned embers. Vedic chants came to a standstill and the planet shook at the loud cry of Sati. "No one in any universe has ever dared to speak of Shiva like this. Fie on me for hearing such words about him. You will repent this, Daksha."

Thus, in that very moment, Sati invoked her latent energy and turned her body into a mound of ash. The *devas* trembled. The haughty Daksha was scared too but he did not show it.

"Daksha," Brihaspati spoke solemnly, "everything you've ever known will come to an end now."

"Huh, what can that one man army do? I will–"

Brihaspati raised his arm signaling Daksha to stop because he did not want to hear anything degrading about Shiva, for he had become Brihaspati, the wisest of all, by the grace of Shiva.

The *ganas*, who had accompanied Sati, hurried back to Kailasha at the speed of light and eulogized Shiva to bring him out of his deep *dhyana*. Shiva gently opened his long eyes. They prostrated before him and in great fear narrated what had transpired at Daksha's *yajna*.

Shiva rose from his seat in great fury. His right hand reached his head, from where he pulled one strand of his matted locks and flung it on the ground. A mammoth figure rose as soon as the lock hit the ground. It was Virabhadra, a terrifying *gana* of Shiva. Dark like coal Virabhadra had eight hands, each one holding a weapon.

Still livid, Shiva took out one more lock and pitched it on the ground. This time arose Bhadrakali, the wrathful and terrifying form of Devi. Dark like the night of *amavasya*, she had 18 hands holding conch, discus, lotus, mace, trident, lance, scimitar, sword, thunderbolt, a demon's head, goblet, goad, waterpot, cleaver, shield, bow and arrow.

"Annihilate!" Shiva commanded and pointed in the direction of Daksha's *yajna*.

He picked up his *damaru* and began playing it wildly. Birds hid in their nests, does and cows had miscarriages, trees fell, oceans swelled, and with each strike of the *damaru* random energies began manifesting. Bhadrakali ululated, mountains split in two and glaciers broke. Eight devis, companion energies of the Supreme Goddess, appeared to assist her in the battle. They were: Kali, Katyayani, Chamundai, Ishaani, Mundamardini, Bhadra, Vaishnavi and Twarita.

Shiva, the Nataraja, began the cosmic dance of destruction, and not before long, countless *ganas* assumed wrathful and terrifying forms.

"*Har Har* Mahadev," they bellowed.

Virabhadra and Bhadrakali, with *ganas* in tow, arrived at Daksha's *yajna* and destroyed everyone and everything that came in their way. Many *devas* fled and many took to hiding. Some tried to combat but didn't last more than a millionth fraction of a moment. The rest of the *devas* knew that it was worthless, if not altogether pointless, to fight against Shiva, even if it were for Daksha, the Prajapati. Shiva's legions continued the rampant destruction like wild elephants running amok in a garden of tender flowers. They were not after the *devas* but Daksha. It was his condescending behavior that had enraged Sati and Shiva. It was Daksha's arrogance that had taken away their revered Goddess from them.

Virabhadra spotted Daksha who was ordering his troops to charge. In one giant leap, Virabhadra reached him. Standing before him, without uttering a word or a warning, obeying Shiva's order, he decapitated Daksha in one effortless stroke. But the *ganas* continued with the destruction.

Fearing that this might be the end of time, the *devas*, along with their retinues, approached Shiva and sang eulogies of his kind heart and glories. A few moments later, that would be a few thousand years on our Earth, Shiva calmed down but he did not speak to anyone. Virabhadra, Bhadrakali, other devis and *ganas* merged back with Shiva's form and he sat there in a sombre mood.

The *devas* were aware that only Shiva could restore harmony and he would have to do it before he assumed his yogic posture, for Shiva's *dhyana* could last for thousands of years. They pleaded him to forgive Daksha. At their bidding, Shiva went to the site of *yajna*.

It had become a bloody battlefield. Uncountable gods, their entourage, horses, elephants lay there slain. Queen Prasuti fell at Shiva's feet and begged that her husband be brought back to life. Shiva lifted her up because she was Sati's mother after all. He looked around and saw where Daksha's head was crushed and mashed; Virbhadra had stomped on it. It was only the crown next to it that gave away it was Daksha's head.

Shiva took the head of a sacrificial goat and placed it on Daksha's body, thus bringing him back to life. He rubbed his hand on his body to take a bit of ash and blew it in the air. All those who had been slain came back to life; all but Sati. Shiva knew that Sati wanted to be pure for him again after having violated her *pativrata* dharma by arguing with him, the omniscient Shiva. He knew that it would be a few thousand years before Sati will be reborn as Parvati and perform intense penance to be his consort once again.

Shiva went back to Kailasha, sat in his yogic posture and took the deepest plunge into *dhyana*, taking his meditative trance to nearly a point of no return.

THE BIRTH OF PARVATI

As time ticked by, a demon called Tarakasura began conquering *devaloka* and all the other planes of existence. He was too powerful, invincible. For thousands of years he had sat in such searing *tapasya* that Brahma had to appear before him. Daksha's *yajna* had already been destroyed. Tarakasura knew that Sati had given up her life and that Shiva would not take anyone else as his consort. Therefore, he asked Brahma for a boon that he could only be killed by a son of Shiva.

The Supreme Goddess, Sati was reborn as Parvati to Himavan, the king of the Himalayas or the Himalayas himself, and Mena, a celestial nymph and the queen of Himavan. Parvati did intense *tapasya* and received Shiva as her husband. Himavan, unlike Daksha, was a humble and just king. He accepted his daughter's choice wholeheartedly. Soon after Shiva took Parvati as his consort, the natural yogi that he was went back into his meditative state.

The *devas* were aghast because they needed Shiva to consummate the bond with Parvati so that she could bear his son, who would have eventually slain Tarakasura. But who could awaken Shiva from his *dhyana*? They sank to their knees in supplication and begged Parvati to intervene in Shiva's *dhyana* and bring him to the normal plane of consciousness. When she heard the cause, she said shyly that no *pativrata* woman would break her husband's meditation for a sexual union. Besides, she knew that if Shiva had thought it right, he would have done so long time ago.

"Pray to him," she suggested, "he'll give you the right thought to emerge victorious."

The *devas* did as instructed, but after a while a thought entered their minds. They sent Manamatha, the god of love, who shot his five shafts of love to rouse the desire of copulation in Shiva. When those arrows hit Shiva, he was utterly displeased. He opened his third eye and turned Manamatha to ashes. Suddenly, the whole world became a desolate place. Love became dry as no man wanted to touch any woman and vice-versa. The birds and animals stopped breeding as there was no desire in the absence of Manamatha.

The *devas* approached Shiva along with Rati, the wife of Manamatha, and begged Shiva to restore Manamatha to his physical form. Manamatha, however, had already been turned to ashes. Shiva granted a boon that since Manamatha could not be brought back to life, he would now live *ananga*, without form, in all living entities and keep desire alive. Rati pleaded with Shiva to at least cast his yogic glance at the mound of ash so that Manamatha could be delivered.

Shiva hesitated but when Rati wouldn't relent, he agreed to cast a glance at the knoll of ash. As soon as he did that, a form arose from the ash. It was Bhandasura, another demon, who made his abode in Shonitpura. He wreaked even greater havoc on the *devas*. Distraught and lost, they approached the eternal itinerant, Narada, who advised them to do a *yajna*.

"It all started from a *yajna*," the sage said. "It'll end with a *yajna*. Only the Supreme Goddess can help now."

The *devas* organized an elaborate *yajna* and out of its sacrificial fire the Supreme Goddess arose in the form of Maha Tripura Sundari. This was an exquisite form: fair colored, four-armed, fragrant, heady, beautiful, well-endowed, compassionate yet she was holding the five arrows of cupid, a goad, a bow and an arrow.

The *devas* didn't know how to propitiate her. Confessing their ignorance, they begged Devi to explain how to welcome her. Mother Divine called upon her eight companion energies called *vagadevis*. They were the same who had manifested at the time of Bhadrakali's origin. They had been a witness to various aspects of Devi.

The *vagadevis* began singing glories of the Supreme Goddess by addressing her with her one thousand names, which are also known as *Lalita Sahasranama*. They began most reverently and melodiously:

> "Om śrīmātā śrīmahārājñī śrīmat-sinhāsanēśvarī, cidagni-kuṇḍa-sambhūtā dēvakārya samudayatā."
>
> (*Lalita Sahasranama*, 1)
>
> O Devi, the sacred mother, You are the eternal providence whose refuge we seek, you are the empress of all worlds, most gloriously seated in your throne, O mother you only manifest to fulfil noble intentions arising out of the fire of purity in one's mind.

The eight *vagadevis* went on to sing glories of Devi. And this is where, in *Lalita Sahasranama*, the first mention of kundalini and chakra is ever made. Before all other scriptures, commentaries, *samhitas*, this is where kundalini is first touched upon as the pristine formless aspect of Goddess, the primordial energy.

☥

I do not let my words scatter here and there like pollen, nor do my sentences grow like purposeless weeds. I have carefully, cautiously and consciously chosen to give you the background story of kundalini because between Daksha's *yajna* and manifestation of Devi, lies the secret of the *sadhana* of *chakras*.

There is not a classical text on chakras that I haven't examined but, not surprisingly, I found them lacking in practical and esoteric aspects. If you are merely interested in theoretical exposition, you may gain more by reading such texts. Hence, disregarding pure theoretical knowledge and contemporary texts, I have based this entire treatise on *Lalita Sahasranama* alone because all hurdles and milestones of kundalini *sadhana* are present in this legend, like butter exists in milk.

My words in this book are only for those who are not just interested in reading but actually experiencing the truth of kundalini themselves.

As for me, I've prayed to Devi in her formed and formless aspects for more than two decades. I have invoked her in the tantric way and the Vedic way. I have seen her, I have been her, and I have seated her in my very being. In the Himalayan woods, on cremation grounds, in caves, under trees, and in abandoned places, I've played in her motherly lap, I've sported with her youthful form. If you doubt that this is possible then I encourage you to put this book down and read something that is more believable, maybe today's newspaper or something else that your conscious mind can accept and understand.

This work is based on my direct experience and I'm presenting you the truth of the chakras as it is, without any sugar coating or exaggeration.

Lalita Sahasranama was then narrated by Hayagriva, a form of Vishnu with the head of a horse, to the sage Agastya for the benefit of human race on this planet and many other parallel ones. So, what you have in this book is straight from the horse's mouth, if you see what I mean.

All glories to Devi!

THE FIRST PRACTITIONER

With boundless enthusiasm and reverence, Lord Hayagriva narrated the glories of Devi in the form of *Lalita Sahasranama*. The great sage Agastya was filled with veneration as he was drenched in his own tears. He sought Lord's blessings so he could do intense *tapasya* and eternally behold the divine form of Devi in his mind's eye.

"So be it," Hayagriva said and granted him the privilege to chant the thousand names of Devi. Sage Agastya was the first to be initiated in the chanting of *Lalita Sahasranama*. He knew that without initiation, he was like a seedless fruit – complete but incapable of further evolution.

Agastya bowed before his guru Hayagriva in deep gratitude and reverence.

"But," Hayagriva warned, "the *sadhana* of Devi is incomplete without tantra and Shiva alone can give you that esoteric knowledge."

He instructed Agastya to meditate on the thousand names of the Supreme Goddess, devoting one *ayana*, six months, to each name and thus completing his meditation over a period of five hundred years. It was only after such profound meditation, he said, that Shiva would impart him the complete *sadhana* of Devi.

Agastya was eager but he knew that like everything in nature, *sadhana* is an organic process. It comes to fruition in its own time. It can't be rushed. He took *padadhuli*, dust from the Lord's feet and sprinkled some on his dreadlocks and rubbed the rest on his forehead.

Agastya began meditating on Devi with single-pointed concentration. Every time he realized the true meaning of her name, tears would roll down from his eyes. Sometimes, he would laugh hysterically, and sometimes, he would go hug wild animals and trees, for he saw Devi alone in everything and everyone. The more he meditated on her divine names the more he revered her.

Seasons came and seasons went, tiny seeds had grown into giant trees, sun had travelled *uttarayana* and *dakshinayana* five hundred times. Agastya finished meditating on the thousand names of Devi and had entered in deep absorption.

"O, accomplished one," a dulcet voice spoke, followed by the melodious plucking of vina.

"*Svātmānanda-lavibhūta-brahamādyānanda-santatiḥ,*" Agastya murmured chanting one of the names of Devi as he opened his sloshed eyes, intoxicated from divine love. "O Narada! The bliss one finds from discovering Devi in one's soul is greater than the bliss Brahma can ever have. All other pleasures are like firefly in front of the sun."

He then folded his hands and greeted the wandering saint, and said, "It is my greatest fortune to have your *darshana* at the conclusion of my *sadhana*."

"Narayana, Narayana," Narada said, "your *sadhana* has not concluded, muni, it has only just started."

"O noble sage," Agastya said, "this vessel has gone frail now. I wish to offer it to Devi in a fire offering."

"Narayana, Narayana," Narada laughed and reminded him of Lord Hayagriva's instruction.

Exactly as Hayagriva had asked him, Agastya approached Shiva and prostrated before him. One look at Shiva's radiant and chiseled face, those still eyes, his matted locks flowing down like Himalayan streams, and Agastya forgot all about his old body. He was awashed with vigor and devotion.

Fair-coloured Parvati came and sat near Shiva. Agastya cried, "Devi, O Devi, bless your Agastya, Devi." Torrents of tears rushed from his eyes as he cried like a child and reached out to touch Devi's feet. But, she, the Supreme Goddess, merged in to Shiva in that very moment. Agastya was shocked.

"Where did I lack in my devotion, Mahadev?" he asked with great anxiety. "Why has Devi disappeared?"

"She is beyond appearance and disappearance, O *muni*," Shiva spoke in his deep and sonorous voice, like wind blowing through a Himalayan tunnel. "You have not yet realized the essence of Devi. But, pleased with your devotion and concentration, the time has come that I impart the secrets to you."

Shiva propounded the most mystical knowledge of Devi worship in her formed and formless aspects in both the left-handed and right-handed path of tantra.

"A few thousand years from now, a tenacious and determined sage on earth will complete Devi's *sadhana*," Shiva said in his mystical style without any further disclosure.

Agastya did intense penance over the next one thousand years but only managed to complete the right-handed practices. He went back to Shiva.

"Unlike you, my body is subject to the laws of nature, Mahadev," he said. "I can give up this body and take up a new one but that will be interfering with the dharma of Time. What's the order, my lord?"

"Go and pass on the complete knowledge to Dattatreya on earth and he will give it to Parasurama and Vashistha."

Agastya had a spark of doubt thinking how could Shiva miscalculate. He had clearly said that the *sadhana* of Devi will be done in a few thousand years from now, but it has only been one thousand years, he thought. He knew that all three – Dattatreya, Parasurama or Vasishta – could complete the *sadhana*.

Shiva smiled but said nothing. As instructed, Agastya passed on the esoteric knowledge to Dattatreya and Vasishta, and dropped his own body in Devi *bhava*.

Dattatreya was born from the three aspects of Brahma, Vishnu and Shiva, to the great sage Atri and his wife Anasuya who was famed for her *pativrata* dharma. Dattatreya imparted the *sadhana* to Parasurama but as soon as the complete knowledge was granted, great *vairagya* sprouted in his mind and he did not marry.

Parasurama remained devoted to his guru and never took up a female consort. The *sadhana* could not be completed without the tantric worship with a consort. Dattatreya knew that Parasurama was not just any *rishi* but an incarnation of the Divine himself. He relieved him of the burden of completing Devi *sadhana*.

Parasurama was a Vishnu incarnate on earth who had vowed to rid the planet from tyrant kshatriyas. Other than the occult science of weapons – which he would give to Drona, Bhishma and Karna a few thousand years later – Parasurama never imparted the esoteric *vidya* of Devi to anyone. Vasishta was the only hope now.

It was no secret that Shiva never repeated himself or imparted any *vidya* twice. Dattatreya was not going to give it to any other disciple and if Vasishta didn't do anything with it, the world would forever be deprived of the grace of Devi.

The great sage Vasishta was known to be as old as the sun in earth's solar system. He had seen the rise and fall of kings. He had seen the transition of *yugas*. He had been to the three worlds and fourteen planes of existence. He had seen the transformation of Vishwamitra into a *brahmarishi*. He was not the eager or the impulsive type.

The wise Vasishta saw with his divine eye that the right time had not yet come on earth for anyone, including himself, to practice the *sadhana* of Devi as passed down by Shiva. He also saw how potent it was and that it could be catastrophic in the wrong hands. Even his own son, a sage and a *siddha*, Sakti Muni was not fit to do Devi's *sadhana*, he realized. He clasped the secret of *sadhana* close to his heart and first disclosed it to his grandson Parashara, the one with no desires. A great realization about the futility of the material world dawned on the soft-spoken Parashara as soon as Vasishta finished expounding the *sadhana* to him.

Empowered with the transcendental knowledge, Parashara felt increasingly disconnected from the world. Unlike his father, or grandfather, or sages of the yore, neither did he marry, nor did he keep a consort. Meditating on various aspects of Devi, he spent most of his time in the Himalayas.

The worship of the Supreme Goddess, however, could not be completed without a consort. Immersed in Devi's *bhava*, Parashara did not feel attracted to any woman. Even though he well knew that he had to pass on the esoteric knowledge, he spent most of his life in meditation without worrying about a successor or a worthy recipient.

A few decades passed and Parashara realized that the issue of a successor could not be postponed any further. With that thought in mind he descended from the Himalayas. One day he had to go across Yamuna and the boatman was about to have his meal. He, therefore, asked his daughter, Matsyagandhi, to take the *rishi* to the other side of the river. While she was ferrying him across, Parashara looked up and closed his eyes. With his divine vision, he saw that after more than four thousand years, the stars and planets had aligned themselves most perfectly not just in *Akashganga*, our galaxy, but across many universes. This was the time to spill his seed into a womb to give the world someone who would bring the *vidya* of kundalini to life.

His eyelids lifted gently and he looked at the barely sixteen Matsyagandhi with a sense of desire. There she was in her lissom body, rowing the boat. She was coming of age and her dark skin shone like an ebony tree. It did not matter to the old *rishi* that she smelled like fish. She always did, she was called Matsyagandhi, the one who smells like fish.

Parashara extended his gnarled hand over her young one. Sunrise and sunset never meet but the rays are golden anyway. Unaware, and a little startled, Matsyagandhi looked at the *rishi*'s hand first and then cast her glance in his eyes. This was Parashara. His hypnotic pull was stronger than the earth's gravity. She surrendered and submitted right there, yet she was a bit hesitant for not only she was ovulating, virgin and unwed, it was broad daylight too.

Reading her thoughts, Parashara whispered a mantra and blew in the air. On a nearby island a leaf fell from the tree but before it could reach the ground, clouds appeared out of nowhere and hid the sun. A thick veil of mist arose all around and the shore was no longer visible. It was here that the great *rishi* fathered none other than the legendary Veda Vyasa.

"You will no longer smell like a fisherwoman but a fragrant lotus," he blessed her as he departed, "you will remain *akshata-yoni*, virgin, and your son will be the greatest poet ever to be born in this world." The boat was midway but the *rishi* walked on water to get to the other shore. Destiny had fulfilled its plan and Prashara and Matsyagandhi would never meet again.

A few years later, he established contact with Vyasa to bring to his notice the grand purpose of his life.

THE INITIATION OF VYASA

The young Vyasa, barely seven summers old, sat in rapt attention when the ageing Parashara told him the story of Daksha's *yajna*, manifestation of the Supreme Goddess, penance of Agastya and his passing on the *vidya* at the instruction of Shiva.

Parashara looked around furtively and carefully and in an occult mudra drew a veil of mist, just how he had done when he'd sired Vyasa on Matasyagandhi. The birds stopped tweeting and flew to far off places; deer ran away. Cicada stopped stridulating and the temperature dropped by several degrees so that most small creatures would also vanish.

"No one else must hear of this," Parashara said, and he whispered the *vidya* in its entirety, including the kundalini aspect of Devi, to the young and bright Vyasa.

"You must complete the *sadhana* of Devi," he added, "with her grace, you'll document the most esoteric wisdom for the benefit of the mankind on this planet. She is called Vagavadini, the power of the speech. She'll speak through you. You must create a fourth Veda and include her worship in it. Invoke her with concentration, devotion, discipline and patience and all will become possible."

Vyasa did *dandvatapranama* to his father and vowed to do complete Devi *sadhana*.

"The only goal of my life, father," he said, "is to honor your word."

"The world will eternally sing your glories, my son," Parashara declared proudly. "You will be known as Veda Vyasa."

"All glories to you, my father," Vyasa shouted in ecstasy. "All glories to Devi."

Parashara touched his son's forehead and said, "You are the first on this planet to be initiated into the *sadhana* of kundalini."

Veda Vyasa meditated on the formed aspect of Mother Divine for 12 years and spent the next 12 invoking her as his own latent energy, in the form of kundalini.

As she rose in him, untying the knots and piercing the chakras, Vyasa was filled with light and knowledge. With immense shakti in him, unrestrained and divine, he sat down and composed the greatest epics known to human race. Creating a fourth Veda called *Atharva Veda*, he elucidated tantra and included Devi worship in its secret passages.

Still brimming with wisdom and energy, he composed *Brhamanda Purana* which contains the first documental evidence of *Lalita Sahasranama*. Devi was still working in him and there was nothing that could stop the legendary Vyasa. One after another, he scribed 18 puranas covering every aspect of knowledge, from sublime to mundane, from astrology to tending cows, but Devi was not done yet.

Eventually, he went on to narrate the greatest scripture of all time – *Mahabharata*. The poetic fountain of his supraknowledge was bursting forth so rapidly that no one, not even Vyasa himself, could match the speed. Anyone who chose to write would soon feel tired. So, he called upon Shiva's son, Ganesha, to scribe *Mahabharata*.

Like the thousands of waterfalls cascading down in the Himalayas during the rainy days, countless streams of creativity and wisdom bubbled over in Vyasa's super consciousness. This was not surprising though, for Devi flows in the form of wisdom and grace from a *sadhaka*. The unstoppable Vyasa went on to record *Bhagavada Purana*, the same story, *Amar Katha*, that Shiva had narrated to Parvati once.

Devi appeared before Vyasa, and said, "Your work is complete now, my son. Only you could write this purana. Go rest in my abode eternally." Thus, the Supreme Goddess merged in Vyasa, and Vyasa was never found again.

In kundalini *sadhana*, Vyasa was the first true *sadhaka* on planet earth, and it is our greatest fortune that we have access to *Lalita Sahasranama*, where complete *sadhana* of chakras is strewn like pearls around Devi's neck.

🔱

Somewhere, I hope you do realize that by calling upon Devi and invoking the primordial principle, you too may uncover the same talent as of Vyasa, you too may tap into the same ocean of creativity as he did, and somewhere, you too may join the same rank as Vyasa did. Remember, that all these sages existed like you and I exist now.

Goswami Tulasidasa writes beautifully in *Ramcharit-manas*:

> "Jani ācaraju karu mana māhi, suta tapa tē
>   duralabha kachu nāhi.
> Tapabala tē jaga srjayi bidhātā, tapabala biṣṇu
>   bhayē paritrātā.
> Tapabala sambhu karahi sanhārā, tapa tē agama
>   nahi kachu sansārā."
>   (*Ramcharitmanas*, 1, 162.1-3)

> Don't be surprised dear. Nothing is impossible with tapas. It is with tapas alone that Brahma creates, Vishnu protects, and Shiva destroys. With penance, nothing in the three worlds is unattainable.

It may seem like a tall order, but at the awakening of the kundalini, when you realize who you really are, you will also realize that you are the tallest out there, that there's nothing short or tall as such. If you are willing to walk the path, you will cut through obstacles like water cuts through stones. Your hurdles will vanish like dewdrops do upon sunrise.

This is Devi.

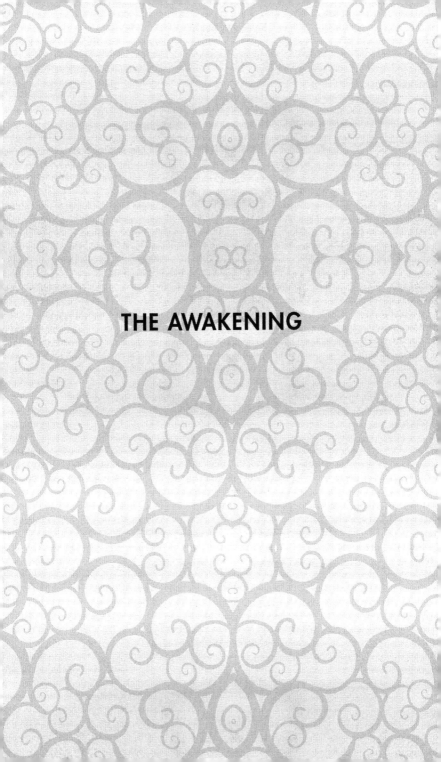

THE AWAKENING

King Kesari, the chief of all primates, and the great queen Anjana, a celestial nymph born on earth due to a curse, sat in searing *tapasya* to have a child. Sun tanned their bodies, snow froze them, mighty winds tried to move them, wild animals posed every threat, but for years, they didn't give up and stood still meditating on the radiant form of Shiva.

Pleased by their devotion and penance, Shiva appeared before them and granted a boon.

"A great son will be born to you," Shiva said in benediction. "He will be wiser than Brihaspati, stronger than Vayu and more radiant than Sun. He won't either drown in water or burn in fire; no weapon of this *loka* or any other will be able to kill him. Eight *siddhis* will serve him like handmaids."

Kesari and his queen stood spellbound, it all seemed too dreamlike – Shiva in his full glory granting a rare boon.

"What's more, O noble king!" Shiva spoke, "he'll be immortal."

"*Namoh Parvati Pataye*," they shouted in ecstasy. "*Har Har Mahadev*."

They fell at his feet and Shiva raised his hand in blessing and disappeared.

The awesome Anjaneya was born. Endowed with boundless power and dexterity, he was wise beyond his years. He would hop from one tree to another covering several miles in one jump. Playing games with other children, he would scare them by growing large like a mountain and then hiding by becoming smaller than an ant. One time he nearly ate the sun thinking it was an orange; *devas* had to intervene.

No one and nothing could contain or even stand his limitless energy. He would root giant trees and fling them like they were straws of *kusha*. This soon became a problem, since he started desecrating *yajnas* and ashrams of great *rishis* in his childlike mischief. When all else failed, they cursed Hanumana that he would forget all his powers. He would only regain them only when someone would remind him of his *siddhis*.

Subsequently, Hanumana began to live like an ordinary *vanara* – clever, wise and spirited, yet ordinary. Everyone heaved a sigh of relief. Many years passed. Rama was born, married to the quiet Sita, exiled for 14 years, Sita was abducted by Ravana and Hanumana met Rama and Lakshmana. One look at Rama and Hanumana became his eternal devotee. The great bear

Jambavaan, older than earth, saw with his farsighted vision that Sita was sitting dejectedly on a small island, in *Ashoka vatika*, a beautiful garden in Ravana's magnificent palace. An ocean separated the island. No boat could go so far. All were in a fix and Hanumana was given the task to deliver Rama's ring to Sita and to convey that *Purushottama* Rama, greatest among all men, would come and free her.

"I'm a simple *vanara*," Hanumana said to Jambavaan and others in Rama's army. "How can I ever reach the island? I don't even know how to swim properly."

Everyone was looking at the vast ocean and clearly realized Hanumana's plight.

"But, you can jump," Jambavaan murmured.

"Jump?" Hanumana exclaimed. "Who can jump across an ocean? It's not a rivulet but an ocean, Jambavaan!"

"Only *you* can," Jambavaan spoke with conviction. "Have you forgotten who you are, Hanumana?"

Hanumana looked at him, confused. Some faint images of his childhood began flashing in front of his eyes, although too distant and too faint to make any sense of.

"You were born from Shiva's boon, Hanumana," Jambavaan spoke in a loud declaration.

Relieving him of the *rishi*'s curse by reminding Hanumana of his powers, Jambavaan continued, "You are not just any *vanara*. Water can't drown you, fire can't burn you, *Anjaneya*! Wake up to the powers you are born with. You can be as giant as the Himalayas or as small as a grain of rye. You can be heavier than the earth or lighter than feather. You can fly faster than the wind itself, you can hop across the oceans, O Hanumana!"

A strange sensation took over Hanumana and images of his childhood became more vivid. He saw how effortlessly he had flown to the sun to eat it, or how he had rooted huge, old trees effortlessly. He remembered how he would cover tens of miles in one jump.

"*Jai* Shri Ram," Hanumana's loud cry nearly brought an earthquake and trees fell. His body began to enormous proportions.

Other *vanaras* reached down to his waist and then knees to eventually look even smaller than his big toe. Hanumana didn't stop, though; he continued becoming bigger and bigger. Soon when he looked down, the colossal army of *vanaras* appeared like a spray of brown dust and Jambavaan looked like a tiny mole, smaller than a black dot.

"*Jai Bajrang Bali, Jai Bajrang Bali*," they shouted with all their might.

"*Jai* Shri Ram," Hanumana thundered louder than the collision of planets, and in one massive jump crossed the entire ocean.

❦

We all are Hanumana – beings of immense power and capabilities. It's not just an aphorism. Our scientific progress validates this. Like Hanumana, our talents are lying latent within us; our potential is waiting to be realized. We are born of a boon and we have forgotten about it, and as a result of that we have taken ordinary ways of life as our destiny. When we get in touch with our reality, our true nature, however, when a Jambavaan reminds us who we really are, we start to grow in our wisdom and conviction. We land on the moon or create supercomputers then. We discover that we are limitless and immeasurable.

This is Kundalini in a nutshell. It is your primal energy, the creative force that wakes you up to your own greatness. Like pearls at the bottom of an ocean, it is lying curled up at the base of your spine.

Kundalini is your polar opposite within you.

When it awakens, you realize how immensely powerful you already are. You experience how there is a whole universe within you. It is your feminine energy if you are a man and your masculine energy if you are a woman. It is your passage, your path to eternal fulfillment within you.

RECOGNIZING THE SUPREME ENERGY WITHIN US

Kundalini is dormant within us because we are made aware of our shortcomings from the moment we are born. We are always compared with someone else out there and we are given examples to become like others. No one tells us that we are good enough; there's always something, some trait, they want us to develop. This conditioning creates a permanent sense of inadequacy in us. To overcome this, we begin our search outside. We start looking for other people who can approve of us, who can endorse us, who can give us a pat on the back. In doing so, we become increasingly distant from our own powers that we were born with.

Why is it that a man feels complete, however briefly, after sexual union with a woman or vice versa? In that letting go, in being yourself, in that union, a sense of security, love and ease arises on its own. In everything that we do, we are relentlessly, even if subconsciously, working towards feeling complete. We drink water when we are thirsty; we eat food when we are hungry. In whatever we feel we lack, nature propels us to take action so we may feel fulfilled.

Some of us go after status, power, fame, wealth and so on to feel that completeness. People continue to go through one broken relationship after another to feel fulfilled. Why is that so? Because, this is how we are made – we feel that we must have someone or something to feel whole. Our true nature is complete, pure; it is bliss. However, our conditioning and demands of this world repeatedly make us feel incomplete, as if we need something or someone else to be happy in our lives.

Like things neither attract nor complete each other though, only opposites complete each other. North doesn't attract north, it attracts south. In this race and struggle to feel complete, we keep attracting the opposite of what we need, of what will actually fulfill us. In doing so, we attract wrong partners, wrong jobs, wrong bosses and so forth.

Awakening of the kundalini is putting an end to attracting the wrong things in our lives. It begins by feeling and experiencing the completeness and fulfillment within us. Piercing of the chakras starts with the realization that 'I am complete', that 'I have everything within me to be happy, to be fulfilled'. It starts by understanding what kundalini really is.

'Talent' is an anagram for 'latent' though. Our talents are latent in us, so to realize them we have to bring them to the fore. Similarly, kundalini, the primal energy, is latent in everyone. The path of awakening the kundalini is to turn inwards and pay attention to our world of emotions, thoughts and talents hidden inside us. It is a deep dive in the ocean of one's existence so one may bring the pearls of character and brilliance to the surface.

All said and done, Kundalini is not a physical reality. Any association of the kundalini with the physical body is ignorant at the best and absurd at the worst. At the rise of the kundalini, there is no snake crawling up your spinal cord. The chakras are not physically there on your body. At the most, they are psychoneurotic plexuses. They are strategically placed wherever there is a concentration of nerves. This does not make the kundalini a mythical concept though. It is your reality, it may not be physical but it is perceptible. The soul cannot be proved, even consciousness for that matter has no physical existence, yet without consciousness we cannot even do the most basic of chores. Similarly, the awakening of the kundalini or piercing of the chakras is as real as the sun, moon and stars.

The sensations you feel during kundalini meditation or the experiences you go through while meditating on the chakras are not unreal or false. They are real, but they are subjective. They only hold meaning for you and not for everyone else. Therefore, absolutizing experiences leads to confusion and conceptualization. You then start aiming for that experience, thinking, "Oh, I must also feel some sensation at the base of my spine to know if I am meditating correctly." This is distracting and deviating you from the real path of meditating on your chakras.

When you sit in a heated room you don't see the heat, but from the warmth you know you are in the presence of heat. Similarly, when you start meditating on the chakras, it is only from your experiences and newly gained abilities that you come to know that a transformation is taking place within you. The greatest transformation upon the awakening of the kundalini is not that you see blinding light (although, that can happen and has happened to me on numerous occasions) or you feel feather-light or you feel highly energetic. These are epiphenomena. This is not the real product; it's more like buttermilk than the actual butter.

The real transformation upon the awakening of kundalini is that you shed your old tendencies and negativity like a snake sheds its old skin. You no longer feel angry or flustered over trivial matters unlike the earlier times. Your emotions and thoughts don't overpower and trample all over you anymore. You begin to gain control of yourself. 'Supranormal' streams of creativity and energy gush forth at the awakening, surprising even you with talents you never thought you had.

There are two more interpretations of this word:

A. KUNDA + LEEN + E

'Kunda' refers to a hole, usually round, in the ground that is meant for gathering and preserving water or fire. Pits for sacrificial fire offerings are called *kunda*. 'Leen' means to be absorbed or attached and 'E' means energy. There's energy that is lying latent, self-absorbed, in a sort of cavity, a nervous plexus, in all human beings. They say Shiva is *shava* (dead body) without *E*. *E* represents energy. Nothing can exist or function without the presence of energy in it, nothing.

Your creative energy is lying at the bottom because you've lost sight of your true nature. As you turn inward and start to meditate on your true nature, this self-absorbed, slumbering, energy begins to rise and with each hurdle it crosses, you feel more powerful than before.

B. THE FEMININE FOR KUNDALA

Kundala means a ring or the coil of a rope. Kundalini, the feminine aspect of your latent energy, is lying coiled. You could imagine to passing water through a twisted pipe instead of a straight pipe.

Our negative views about ourselves, our emotions and attachments have twisted our passage of kundalini. It stands wrung. Just like if you scold a small child, he might just curl up in fear and lie in his bed, kundalini too is curled up and lying down in your root chakra, *muladhara*. It is so because we are almost conditioned to be afraid of ourselves. We are afraid of making mistakes or taking decisions. We are even afraid of doing things right and we want someone else to validate what we have done. In fear, you never sleep with your legs stretched out, you always curl up a bit.

Kundalini's natural abode is the sacral chakra, but it has descended and is lying in the root chakra. These two chakras are sex centres and the greatest guilt most people have in their lives is around their sexual thoughts and acts. Awakening of the kundalini begins with complete acceptance of who you are so that you maybe at ease with yourself. Then you give it attention (meditation) and care, you bring it out of its curled up position to a state of complete acceptance and fearlessness. It no longer remains latent. It becomes potent, a potent instrument to not only fulfilling your dreams but also making you feel whole. Therefore, it is called the formless aspect of Devi, no less divine, no less powerful, no less complete than Mother Divine herself.

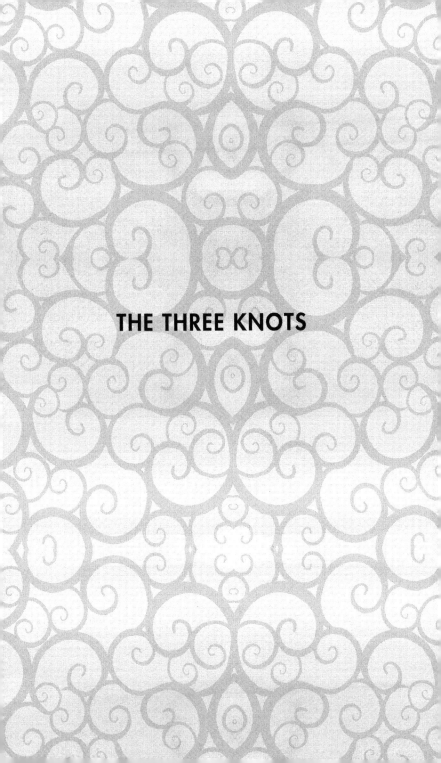

THE THREE KNOTS

Ananda, one of Buddha's chief disciples had served him for decades. He had revered him, looked up to him, loved him and had devoted his whole life to *Tathagata,* the one gone beyond.

"O sage! You've helped so many to gain enlightenment," he said to Buddha one day. "Why is it that I never experience that deep *samadhi* you talk about?"

Buddha smiled and said, "That's because you are still tied to me, Ananda. Untie all knots if you want to experience true awakening."

Ananda was quite puzzled at Buddha's response.

"What are you saying, *Tathagata*?" he said. "If I wouldn't reach the other shore by following you, then how will I? A calf gets home safely when it follows its mother."

"You are already home, Ananda. It is only that you don't realize it. Untie yourself and venture out in the unchartered territories of your mind to know what lies there."

Ananda was dismayed at Buddha's response. He felt he had wasted his whole life because all throughout he had believed that following Buddha meant awakening, but here the sage was telling him the opposite. Three months later, Buddha, at the ripe age of 82, passed away and Ananda was devastated to be left behind. In that great pain of separation and sadness, he sat down to meditate. Hardly a few minutes had passed when he entered into deep trance. In that state of awakening, he had a profound realization: a chain whether of gold or iron is a chain nonetheless. You cannot experience true freedom as long as you are tied to anything at all.

ᛏ

On the path of awakening all knots must be untied. The umbilical cord must be cut if you want to discover an identity of your own. We wouldn't know how deeply we are attached to something till we distance ourselves from it. The process of kundalini awakening or its understanding is incomplete without an intimate knowledge of the three knots that bind each one of us. At every loop, every knot, a rope loses its smoothness. Our knots too make us uneven and they rob us of our smoothness. Just like every knot shortens the rope, our knots truncate our strength and character.

Not coincidentally, in *Lalita Sahasranama*, exposition of kundalini does not start from chakras, but the three knots. There are 182 verses in the *stotra*, out of which 15 are directly linked to the chakras. They mention the *sadhana*, hidden aspects, the nature of chakras, their forms, colors and syllables. But, the first three verses stand independent on their own. They only talk about how the kundalini rises as it pierces the three knots. There is no mention of chakras until much later.

Undoing the knots is a *sadhana* in its own right though, and like any other *sadhana* it's not without hurdles, both within and without.

OVERCOMING HURDLES

There are two types of hurdles in any *sadhana* – external and internal. External hurdles primarily refer to a lack of conducive environment, which includes natural calamities, an unsafe place, lack of social support, non-availability of proper food and so forth. External challenges are of two types: *adi-bhautik*, hurdles that hinder your progress due to lack of resources, and *adi-daivik*, obstacles created by nature, such as storms, wild animals and so on. External challenges are not hard to overcome, you can change your place where your needs are provided for and these challenges disappear.

Here's the thing with external challenges: the more you turn inwards, the less they matter. During my own days of *sadhana* in the woods, the more I intensified my practice, the less external factors mattered. After a while, nothing or no one, from rats to langurs, bothered me any longer. They were there but they ceased to exist for me. As the inner storms, langurs and rats settled down, the ones outside became powerless. No matter whether you are in the woods or in an air-conditioned penthouse, there will be plenty of external hurdles. We can't let them stop us though. Besides, when compared to the daunting challenges within, the ones without feel like a breeze, a piece of cake.

Internal hurdles as well are further divided into two types: *adi-daihik*, ones that arise from physical ailments in the body, and *adhyatamika*, challenges that block your progress because of thoughts, emotions and desires. *Adi-daihik* could be asthma, arthritis, even common cold or any other disease for that matter. Anything that arises from within your body and disrupts your meditation or focus is an internal hurdle.

A *sadhak*'s main challenge, however, remains to be the internal hurdles of the second type – *adhyatamika*. This is where the three knots come into play. They are called *Brahma Granthi, Vishnu Granthi* and *Rudra Granthi*. Among the three of them, they cover the whole spectrum of inner challenges that any *sadhak* encounters on the path of awakening of the kundalini.

For the most part of our lives, we are battling with ourselves. We try hard to resist certain unwholesome emotions, thoughts and desires and we try very hard to cultivate some desirable ones. We want to forgive certain people, but feel guilty because we can't let go off the hurt they caused us. We want to be happy, we don't want to feel hatred for anyone or be lustful, yet it seems that our emotions and thoughts have a life of their own.

We are trying to persuade our feelings and thoughts, we want to strike a friendship but they don't seem to be interested. In retaliation, rather than understanding, we begin resisting them, we start avoiding them. This resistance turns into a knot and it complicates our lives. Our knots, they tie us, trip us and shorten us.

> "mūlādhāraikanilayā brahmagranthivibhedinī,
> maṇipūrāntaruditā viṣṇugranthivibhedinī.
> ājñācakrāntarālasthā rudragranthivibhedinī,
> sahasrārāmbujārūḍhā sudhāsārābhivarṣiṇī.
> taḍillatāsamarucihṣaṭcakroparisaṃsthitā,
> mahāśaktiḥ kuṇḍalinī bisatantutanīyasī."
>
> (Lalita Sahasranama, 38-40)

From *muladhara*, the root chakra, kundalini moves pierces the Brahma knot in the *Swadishthana*, the sacral chakra, goes through the solar plexus and pierces the *Vishnu Granthi* in the heart chakra continuing straight through throat and brows, it pierces the *Rudra Granthi* in the head. There it meets with the thousand-petaled lotus and enjoys a shower of bliss and divine intoxication.

The nature of kundalini is like the batteries of lightening and flashes as it rises above the six chakras. Completely drunk with the nectar, its form is subtler than even a fraction of the billionth part of a strand peeled from the lotus stem.

When you are filled with positivity and light, when you start to see the 'real you', you bloom on your own, it's effortless. And when you blossom and open up, the knots loosen and then disappear. As you evolve spiritually and progress on the path, these knots begin to untie themselves just like lotuses open on their own when sunbeams caress them. In the actual process of kundalini awakening, you don't have to focus on any of the knots as such. There is no visualization of untying them as well.

When knots are formed with a muscle spasm, you just let it be; you massage it tenderly and it goes away. Similarly, when you gently massage your soul, it starts to relax, you begin to be at perfect ease with yourself, with how, what, who and where you are on the journey of life – this is the beginning of kundalini awakening.

In the Hindu tradition, Brahma's job is to create, Vishnu's role is to sustain and Rudra or Shiva's job is to terminate. These are the three roles that also tie us down. The desire to create is *Brahma Granthi*, the desire to hold on is *Vishnu Granthi* and the desire to get rid of what you don't like is *Rudra Granthi*. Respectively, they also represent three major elements of human life: sex, emotions (positive and negative) and destructive thoughts. Let me delve deeper into them.

BRAHMA GRANTHI

Brahma represents creation and also the aspect of procreation. Therefore, not by coincidence, the knot of Brahma is in the sacral chakra, your genitals more specifically. Kundalini starts from the root chakra, at the base of spine – that is where the greatest concentration of nerves lies.

The strongest desire in any individual is the desire to create, because this desire is directly linked to a release of the creative energy in you. You can call it sex. Sex is not merely satiating your lust, it is your most creative aspect. Nature compels you, impels you and propels you to constantly find avenues where this creative energy may be used. Nature's only dharma is growth and every creature in this existence is primed accordingly.

The first challenge for any practitioner is to rise above sexual thoughts and desires. By that I do not mean that you observe lifelong abstinence. You may have to practice it, though, in the initial stages. Abstinence is recommended purely from the view of channelizing your thoughts. You can better control your mind when you know you can't just have something for a certain period of time.

It's like when you are trying to write an important letter or an article and an email flashes on your screen. Your friend has shared a link with you and as soon as you click on that link you are taken to a news website. You finish reading the article and at the bottom, there are suggestions for other relevant articles. You click on one of them and start reading it. That article contains another link, you click on that and off you go to another website. Before you know it, three hours have been wasted and you still haven't finished writing the important letter you had sit down to complete in the first place. Imagine if you had gone offline while writing that letter, there would have been no distractions. Abstinence is something like that. It's going offline for a period of time so you can concentrate better on what you have to do.

I do not endorse or see merit in lifelong continence because I find it unnecessary and unnatural. I have met countless celibate monks and not even one of them was actually happy being a celibate, they all struggled with it. So, what do I mean by rising above sex? You have to be completely comfortable, at perfect ease, with your sexuality and your sexual orientation.

During the *sadhana*, you will have a barrage of thoughts – sensual, sexual, taboo, perverted, and so on. Let them come, don't react to them; you simply carry on with your meditation on the chakra of your present focus. You did not choose your sexual orientation; you did not choose your sexual thoughts. You were born with them. The more you stop reacting and chasing your thoughts, the less they will bother you.

I remember that while growing up, there was an old man and the young children used to tease him because he would react vehemently. He would take his stick and run after them. They would ridicule him (I know it was absolutely cruel). They only provoked him to solicit that reaction from him. One time he went away for a pilgrimage and returned after several months. Soon after, he stopped reacting and within weeks the children stopped poking fun at him. When you don't react, a sense of ease arises. Resistance goes away. When you resist something, you have to exert double the force, it is exhausting and demoralizing.

Think of abstinence as keeping a fast, when your mind knows, "I have to stay hungry for nine days," let's say. On the first day, you can get through just fine. On the second day, it'll be a bit harder. On the next four days, it will be even harder. You will find yourself thinking about food most of the time. In the last three days, you will be counting moments, thinking to yourself, "Only a few days to go" and so on. At the end of nine days, when you will have the opportunity of having food, chances are that you will end up eating in excess. Like normal food, sex too is a food for body and mind.

Once a man visited me. He was in his mid-seventies. He was quite perturbed by the fact that he still had sexual thoughts and was active sexually. He felt guilty about it.

He said, "I retired years ago and still I have sexual thoughts."

"It's okay," I said, "your body and reproductive organs don't know that you are retired."

"Sex too is food," I added, "as long as you are eating food, your body will want sex too. Mind never retires."

"So, it doesn't make me a bad person, right?"

"On the contrary, it means you are normal," I said, "no reason to feel guilty about something you didn't choose."

Mind doesn't care whether you are retired from the service or you are a senior citizen; it's alive as ever. Just like you may have the desire of eating fine food or wearing nice clothes, or going out etc., you have sexual thoughts. If you don't give them extra importance, they are just like other thoughts – they emerge, stay for a moment and then disappear.

All said and done, *Brahma Granthi* is not merely the sexual knot, for Brahma doesn't just represent procreation but creation too. If sex alone was enough to harness our creative energies, we wouldn't be in such a rat race today. No matter how rich or poor one is, whether a millionaire or a billionaire, a local minister or the Prime Minister, everyone is busy in wanting and acquiring greater share of everything they can have. They want to create, do something more than what they have already done. And this is the second aspect of this knot: to create.

Brahma Granthi represents creation, expansion and multiplication. There is no doubt that millions out there need to work very hard all day to support themselves. At the same time, however, there are millions who are incessantly working towards amassing wealth, eyeing promotions, bigger houses, bigger cars, and so on. They work hard to earn more, then they spend more, and then they work even harder to earn much more so they can support their spending. It seems to be the wisdom and way of the twenty-first century.

I'm not suggesting this is good or bad; it's your

personal choice. While doing chakra *sadhana*, the second temptation to resist is the desire to have more. It begins by taking a good look at what all you are already blessed with and by pursuing any material objective with a sense of awareness. Gratitude and mindfulness are like chopsticks. You need both to hold the food of temptation.

As a *sadhak* progresses and rises above his sexual thoughts and thoughts of creation, a kind of stillness starts to brew in his mind, undercurrents of restlessness subside and a sense of gratitude arises naturally. "Truly, I have everything" – this feeling begins to carve a place in your mind. Just like a fully bloomed flower attracts bees naturally, a mind that has gone beyond creation and procreation attracts thoughts of a different nature. Tangled in the second knot now, different desires sprout in the mind.

VISHNU GRANTHI

Somewhere the root cause of our suffering is a deep desire for permanence. We are not comfortable with the transient nature of this world. We find it hard to believe that everything is temporary. We want our joys, pleasures and attainments to be eternal. We don't want to lose our loved ones and if we could, we would have them by our side always. The desire to hold on, to not let go, whatever we have acquired is one of the strongest desires.

Such a desire though limits us greatly, it restricts us and it ties us down. This is the second knot – *Vishnu Granthi*. Vishnu's seat is in the heart chakra.

Based on our desire to be eternally happy, we continue working hard and doing things to ensure that we don't lose. This clinging is the seed of all emotions, and emotions are the second greatest hurdle for any practitioner. While meditating when you try to quiet your mind, that's when you become most aware of your emotions. They are not just either positive or negative emotions but a mixture of both, for emotions are simply those thoughts that didn't abandon and now they have found a place in your heart. You go through regret, repentance, guilt, anger, hatred, jealousy, envy, joy, peace and many others.

When you let your thoughts brew and not abandon them, they become desires or emotions. Vishnu sustains the creation. Your desires and emotions are the basis of your living. Think about it for a moment – most of us are mostly working towards fulfilling towards what we desire or care about. The knot of desires and emotions represent the second hurdle for any sincere seeker.

Should you let go of desires and not have emotions? The truth is desires and emotions make us human; they make us who we are. It is not possible to completely let go of either the desires or the emotions. You may not have big desires of making a lot of money or becoming really famous and so on, but that does not mean you are free of desire.

The desire to eat something different today, the desire to speak to your loved ones, the desire to watch a movie, the desire to entertain yourself – they are all desires. The harder you have to work towards fulfilling a certain desire, the greater is the joy that you are likely to experience upon its fulfillment. It does not mean the joy will be everlasting or even long-lived. It simply means the surge of joy you experience is greater when you have to work harder or longer towards its attainment.

How we accept what comes to us greatly determines our emotional state and such state in return largely affects our response to those situations. Someone criticizes you and you are unable to accept or reject it. It will trigger a negative emotion in you. It might make you feel down or you might loathe the criticizer. In that state of mind, you may say or do something that you wouldn't normally do. If, however, you are able to either reject the criticism outright, quietly in your mind, or accept it and flush it out of your system, you will not experience the swelling of any negativity in you. It is easier to swim in a pond than in a whirlpool. When you understand that you don't have to react to your emotions or thoughts while you are meditating on chakras, they become less intense. As their intensity decreases, they no longer remain a whirlpool but become a silent pond and then you see what lies at the bottom. Everything becomes crystal clear.

Your emotions may cause momentary ripples but they wouldn't be able to become giant whirlpools. As you rise above your sexual thoughts and become somewhat indifferent to your emotions, you start to see the residue. A final and third category of thoughts come and disrupt your meditation.

RUDRA GRANTHI

There comes a stage in the life of a serious meditator when he is no longer struggling with sexual thoughts, when they no longer have any negative feelings towards anyone else. There comes a phase when they are actually grateful. Just as the mind starts to experience stillness, just when they begin to see the colours at the bottom of the reef, they are caught unaware by another wave of thoughts. No, these thoughts are not about having more or building more, they are not about harming anyone, these are much worse. These are self-deprecating thoughts that leaves the meditator vulnerable. They make you feel as if you are inadequate, as if you wouldn't ever get there. Your weak moments, or failures of the past, begin to flash in your inner eye and all you see is what all you lack as opposed to what you have within you.

The third knot is the knot of thoughts called *Rudra Granthi*. It is just after the *agya* chakra, the brow plexus. Shiva's role is destruction; not necessarily in the form of annihilation but termination. Untying this knot is a two-stage process. In the first one, you go beyond your destructive thoughts; you realize that you don't have to hold onto your past, you understand that you can't allow your yesterday to ruin your today. As you meditate with that awareness and commitment, destructive thoughts fly away like frightened birds do at the sound of a loud clap. The second stage is a realization that all thoughts are empty in their own right. They are devoid of any essence, that if I don't give them importance they can't do anything on their own. If you observe carefully, you'll notice that all visible phenomena have a point of origin, a life of certain duration, and a point of termination. The knot is in the brain because as they say, it's all in your head. You may experience certain emotions, you may have desires, and you may long for physical intimacy. If you are able to terminate the thought in your head though, the desire or emotion will disappear like it never existed.

This is the hardest knot to untie, the greatest hoop you have to get through. *Rudra Granthi* also refers to the onslaught of thoughts you experience while meditating on the chakras. This is also the last stage of kundalini awakening and the most intense one too. Meditating with unflinching focus and determination, the practitioner has to become a yogi like Shiva to undo this knot. As you progress, you start to become aware of your thoughts effortlessly. Just like a bird can naturally fly and a fish can naturally swim, you become naturally aware.

No matter how hard or how badly entangled is a knot, you can't loosen it by pulling on it. Frustration or intolerance has no role or room in kundalini meditation. A serious practitioner knows that he or she must be extremely patient. We have to examine the knot and then untie it with firm but relaxed hands. That's how you need to look upon *Brahma, Vishnu and Rudra Granthi*. Some examination, a bit of observation, a lot of patience and a great deal of effort to untie is required. No knot is hard enough then. If you walk the path and not give up, you will get the results exactly as expected.

That is why I don't call it the philosophy but the science of chakras. It has a definitive cause and effect relationship. Nothing is without a cause-and-effect in the divine play. Everything is beautifully interlinked, interdependent and impartial.

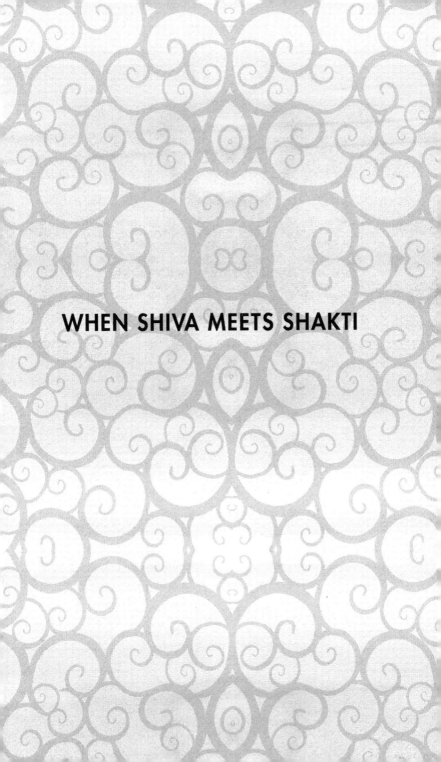

WHEN SHIVA MEETS SHAKTI

Afew hundred million years ago, when continents on earth were not separated by oceans but existed as only one supercontinent, a valiant and powerful king called Susena ruled there. To spread his empire far and wide and to establish himself as a *chakravartin*, a world emperor, his royal counsel advised him to do *ashvamedha yajna*.

Ashvamedha yajna or horse-sacrifice was undertaken only by the greatest of the great kings to demonstrate their sovereignty over all other states and rulers. A royal steed was let loose and the king's retinue would follow the horse. Wherever it would roam, that area would come under the command of the king. If any other ruler challenged the new sovereign by holding the horse captive, there ensued a bloody battle.

Susena's horse covered great distances and no other king dared to challenge him. Several weeks passed and his territory expanded to many new states. One day, the horse stopped to drink water from a pond which was in a secluded ashram in a forest, next to a giant mountain called *Ganda*. Only a few yards away from the pond was an old banyan tree, its periphery stretching several tens of cubits. Under the tree sat a radiant *rishi*, unmoving, in deep *samadhi*. His name was Gana.

Unaware, Gana sat still like a rock, his kundalini latched to his *sahasrara* and drinking nectar like a child suckles his mother's breast. Various ministers of the king, who were part of the retinue and following the horse, camped in shade, next to the pond, without paying their respects to the great *rishi*. With a view to relax, they opened bottles of wine and began conversing with each other. A few hundred soldiers pitched their tents a little away.

Gana's son, a great a *tapasvin* and a *rishi* himself, saw all this as arrogance and intrusion. He could not bear the disrespect shown to his father.

"O foolish men!," he roared. "You are drunk on pride like your king. Go tell him that I've captured his horse."

The ministers didn't take the slur too well and immediately ordered their soldiers to arrest him.

The young *rishi* whispered the mystical mantra of the devi Jaya, and turned advancing soldiers into a mound of ashes. All this happened too fast, some of the ministers were still mounting their horses. Trembling with fear, they fell at his feet and sought his forgiveness. He didn't utter a word though and just walked into the mountain with the royal horse and disappeared like soul does at the time of death. They paid their obeisance to Gana, who was still in deep *samadhi*, and went back to their king.

Susena heard the whole story and instructed his younger brother Mahasena, known for his wisdom and valour, to approach the *rishi* with the greatest humility and beg his pardon.

"Don't take any troops with you," he said. "Go like a seeker."

Mahasena immediately left for the ashram and reached there a few weeks later; the *rishi* was still in *samadhi*. His son was standing a little away guarding his father like eyelids guard the eyes. Mahasena did a full length prostration in front of the *rishi* and placed a basket of fragrant flowers, dry fruits, sweetmeats along with a shawl of silk. He then folded his hands and sat there in waiting.

Gana's son was pleased with the demeanor of *Mahasena*.

"What do you seek, O noble one?" he said. "I'm his son."

Mahasena offered his obeisance to the young sage as well, and spoke in a low voice, "I wish to speak to your father, if I may."

"I too can grant you whatever you can imagine," the young *rishi* said. "I give you my word."

"I'm eternally grateful to you," Mahasena replied. "Please grant me an audience with your father today."

"My father is in *kevalanirvikalpa samadhi*," he replied. "Piercing all the chakras, his kundalini has reached *sahasrara* and he sits above and beyond all the physical elements and needs of his body. He will not come out of this state for twelve years. Nearly five have passed and seven remain."

"But, since I've already given you my word," he added. "I'll do transference of thought that will cause a ripple in his state of superconsciousness."

The young *rishi* sat cross-legged and began an intense meditation. A *muhurta*, forty-eight minutes, later he looked at Mahasena, and said, "My father has become aware of his mind now, he'll open his eyes any moment."

Hardly had he completed his sentence when Gana spoke in a soft voice, "May you live long, Mahasena."

Mahasena clasped the *rishi*'s feet and pleaded guilty on behalf of the state.

Gana reproached his son for acting recklessly and instructed him to immediately release the horse. Bowing before his father in apology and remorse, he went towards the mountain, vanished and emerged with the horse a few moments later.

Mahasena pinched himself and rubbed his eyes to make sure he wasn't dreaming. More interested in the unthinkable he had just seen than the horse, he asked the young *rishi*, "O great *tapasvin*, I just saw you disappear into the mountain and then manifest yourself out of thin air."

"Show him your mountain," Gana said with an all-knowing smile, mischievous like a child's. "His is a long life."

Tethering the horse outside, the young *rishi* took Mahasena close to the mountain.

Mahasena stood there dumbfounded as the *rishi*'s son said, "Come, let's enter."

"Enter where? How?" he thought, for there was no door.

Reading his mind, the young sage said, "This is my creation and you'll have to be in my state of consciousness to experience my world."

Saying this, he entered into the mind of Mahasena and triggered an expansion of consciousness. Soon, Mahasena didn't see his body as one solid block but a colony of billions of tiny units, each one was simply a passage of energy; each one *was* energy, in fact. Effortlessly, he followed the young *rishi* and both entered inside the mountain.

Mahasena was startled beyond what words can ever express. This was not just a mountain from the inside, it was a whole universe. There were billions of twinkling stars, a moon, rivers, mountains, trees, birds, fishes, mammals and reptiles; it had everything in it. It was a vast creation.

They travelled at the speed of light from one location to another, night gave way to day and sun arose unearthing the beauty of the *rishi*'s creation. Mahasena even felt scared looking at the vastness. He thought that he would get lost. He held onto the young *rishi* as they travelled across oceans and endless forests. A whole day went by but Mahasena felt neither hunger nor tiredness.

"We should leave now," the *rishi* said.

"It's so amazing here," Mahasena exclaimed. "It's another universe. Can we not stay one more day, please?"

The *rishi* laughed. "Mahasena," he whispered, "trust me, we should go."

Obeying the young sage, Mahasena followed him and soon they were out of the mountain.

Everything looked different outside. Only the old tree stood where Gana, the great *rishi*, still sat in *tapasya*. Other than that, there was no pond, but a mighty river flowing there. The horse was nowhere to be seen. The trees looked a lot different, some almost looked ancient, even the animals and apes were not what they were a day ago.

"Where are we?" Mahasena asked. "I can see the great *rishi* but this place looks different."

"It's the same place," the *rishi* replied.

"How can it change so much in just one day?" he asked in disbelief, even doubting that perhaps the young sage was frolicking with one of his tricks.

Gana's son laughed, and then said most seriously, "Mahasena, time is relative. My universe runs on a different wheel of time than yours."

Mahasena looked bewildered, like a child lost in a fair. He could not fathom any of what the young *rishi* was telling him.

Realizing his predicament, he clarified, "Mahasena, twelve thousand years have passed on earth."

"Twelve thousand years!"

"Yes. One day in my universe is equivalent of twelve thousand years here."

"What about my brother, my wife, children, the kingdom?" Mahasena said as if he just woke up from a dream, a feeling that wasn't entirely incorrect.

"They are all gone, Mahasena," the *rishi* said. "The wheel of time never stops for anyone."

Mahasena dropped right there like a creeper without support, and putting his head between his hands, he began crying like a child.

"Listen, Mahasena," the young *rishi* said. "Who and what are you crying for? Nothing here is permanent. Earth, stars, sun, universe, your siblings, family, your body, or anything you can touch, see, smell, hear or feel – none of this is eternal, Mahasena.

"No one is dying or living, it's one big illusion. Don't you see? You think that even my universe was real? It was simply a creation of my consciousness. Similarly, this world too is a creation of collective consciousness. Look at my father, he's still there, even thousands of years later, because he has tapped into the source of his energy. There is no movement there, and therefore there is no change or decay."

His words worked like balm on the wounded mind of Mahasena and he stopped crying. He felt calm, like a thirsty traveller feels in the desert upon drinking pure water.

"Mind becomes eternal when it becomes still," the *rishi* continued. "No change is possible without movement. Truth is still, and that's why it's eternal."

"Please help me see the truth, O *rishi*!" Mahasena fell at the feet of the young sage.

"Anything you can see, hear, touch, smell or feel is not the truth, O wise one," he replied. "Truth can't be seen, truth must be experienced. It dawns like sunrise upon earth."

"What must I do to experience the truth?"

"Go and meditate. Awaken your latent energy so you may realize yourself and become the master of your own universe."

Mahasena sat by the *rishi*'s feet as the latter demystified the mysteries of universe and expounded on the three states of consciousness – wakeful, dream and sleep. Empowered with the wise words of the sage and his burning desire to know the truth, Mahasena retired into the forest and began his intense meditation. He meditated till he realized his own true nature. He sat still until the kundalini reached *sahasrara*. Mahasena gained enlightenment by gaining access to his own unconditioned intelligence.

❦

Awakening of the kundalini is realization of your pure abstract intelligence, the type that is not conditioned by your fears, emotions and worries. It is your pristine nature. When you are able to tap into this latent source of energy, you truly become the master of your universe. You can manifest whatever you wish in your life because your scale of consciousness is no longer limited to your body alone; it envelops the whole universe.

If you observe, you'll notice that no matter how hot it may be on any given day, the warm and bright sunlight doesn't burn anything. Objects can become hot, they can even melt, but they don't burn. On the other hand, if you pass sunlight through a lens, the focused beam of light can easily cause a spark in under a minute. This focus, free from dispersion and distraction, turns the same sunlight into an intense beam.

Your kundalini too, as it rises, becomes more intense. From a simple cloud of latent heat at the base of your spine, it begins to transform into a beam and then becomes a more powerful one. By the time, it reaches your *sahasrara*, it gets united with a giant power source. Breaking free of the shackles of thoughts, desires, emotions, fears and phobias, it turns you, the practitioner, into an adept, a *siddha* at whose command anything becomes possible.

The latent energy of the kundalini is present in all of us like fire in wood. Our fears and conditioning hold us back. They plunge our creative energy to the bottom most chakra and we end up using it for petty things for the most part of our lives. And through the years we spend living, majority of the time is spent in either battling with ourselves or with others. There is little sense in fighting with the world or accumulating negativity in our minds. Instead, we have the choice to walk on a path that brings our creativity and energies to the fore.

MASTERING THE MASCULINE AND FEMININE ENERGIES

Each strand of Shiva's matted locks indicates the power of our thought where *sahasrara* are his dreadlocks. With each strand of his hair, a yogi can manifest entities like Virabhadra or Bhadrakali, the masculine or feminine energies, that will work on your behalf to accomplish your goals.

Immolation of Sati is indicative of the power of kundalini, your latent force, that is powerful enough to burn you, the false you. You may wonder, who is the false you? Most of our labels like sister, brother, daughter, son, mother, father, husband, wife, and so on shape us, and dictate our behavior. But, beyond these roles, away from being a man or a woman, beyond even your body, is the purest form of energy, the energy that is the basis of our very existence and potential.

Yogi in his own right is incomplete because yogi can just burn all afflictions and everything. Shiva turned Manmatha, cupid, into ashes. But that is not the longer-term solution because our afflictions too are potent energies. It is only that they are misdirected. Therefore, the key is to channelize, to harness and to regulate. And for that to happen, we must be at ease with our opposites within us.

The union of Shiva and Shakti to produce an offspring, who would have saved the *devas*, represents your immense power that emerges when the kundalini meets *sahasrara*, when your polar opposite joins its source within, for *devas* are your noble intentions. They are ruled by Indra, the chief. The word *indri* means senses and the one who rules the senses is your mind. It gets afraid very easily, it becomes protective and that is why Indra panics whenever anyone sits in *tapasya* because intense meditation completely subdues the talkative mind.

Danavas, or demons, represent our selfish aspect, our excessive self-concern, our negative emotions and our ignoble intentions. It is very easy for distractions, for *danavas* to trump the *devas*, but when a yogi like Shiva unites with Shakti, a state of consciousness arises from that union that wins over the demons. Dharma defeats *adharma*.

Piercing of chakras and awakening of the kundalini is the most responsible enterprise that anyone can undertake for the simple reason that a yogi does not hold the world responsible for his or her feelings and emotions. That has never led anyone to the pinnacle of their potential. A yogi looks within for all answers because if I'm truly the master of my universe then I might as well think, act and be like an emperor.

The first word in *Lalita Sahasranama* is '*Sri Mata*', Mother Divine is my final sanctuary. And like the kundalini, she is within you. The yogi says, "I must seek my own refuge". The next word is '*Srimaharagyi*'. The moment I see and realize myself as my own master, kundalini joins *sahasrara*, she becomes the empress. You then become the owner of your universe.

'*Sri-mat-singhasaneshvari*' is the third name in *Lalita Sahasranama,* and then you sit on your own throne with the greatest grace, conviction and splendor. The fourth name is '*Chid-agni-kunda-sambhuta-deva-karya-samudyta*'. You reach such a level of purity then, that by the mere power of your thought, arising like a spark from the fire pit of a pure mind, you can accomplish the greatest tasks.

When everything is within you, what do you really lack then? When the source of Universe lies latent in you in the form of kundalini, waiting to be shown its way to *sahasrara*, what is that you can't accomplish then? You choose if you want to be arrogant and angry like Daksha or a devotee like Sati, a yogi like Shiva or a seeker like Mahasena, a *rishi* like Gana or his son. These are your choices. Let yourself rise within you and you can be any of these.

'*Uddyata-bhanu-sahasra-abha-chatur-bahur-samanvita*', the fifth name means by holding the four *purusharthas*, endeavours of your life (i.e. *dharma-artha-kama-moksha*), you will radiate with intelligence, wisdom and truth like thousand suns glowing together.

Go! Awaken your potential to realize who you really are. How, you ask?

Now that you know the literal, real and esoteric meaning of chakras and kundalini, let me show you exactly how to awaken this divine energy.

AWAKENING THE GODDESS

THE ACTUAL *SADHANA*

I remember it was snowing outside, very heavily. No birds were chirping, no boars were snorting around my hut, no deers were bleating. Trees were not swaying and winds were not blowing. It was utterly quiet as snowflakes would land softly on the roof of my hut and on the ground outside. There was pin drop silence, perfect quietude for deep meditation. But even the with perfect environment, solitude and silence, my mind was far from being quiet; it was restless.

Several months had passed and even after meditating of a few thousand hours, I had not felt any persistent sensations on my chakras. There was no sign of any kundalini awakening. All I had gained till date was excruciating aches and pains arising from sitting still for extremely long periods, and a constant company of the wild animals.

I sat still while tears continued to trickle down my eyes. The first many drops would simply disappear in my growing beard but eventually as the flow continued, they began landing on my chest. They would roll out warm but end up cold. They interfered with my meditation but I couldn't control them. My palms were resting in my lap and wild rats were playing nearby. They were moving around and about as if they were circumambulating me. It was hardly entertaining. Tears from my eyes continued to fall like raindrops from the sky.

These were not tears of devotion or bliss though. I was crying because I was extremely tired and exhausted. The exhaustion that I had once experienced from running my own business and working in five different time zones was miniscule compared to what I was going through now. This was not just any fatigue, I was tired because I had tried everything I could think of and yet I wasn't any better than when I'd first started.

Ever since I had gone to the Himalayas, I had followed a strict routine of meditation with utmost discipline; never faltering even once. I ate a frugal meal once in twenty-four hours to avoid lethargy. Living in sub-zero temperature for the most part, I bathed every day in icy water. I took only short naps so I could devote all my time to intense meditation.

I slept and sat on the floor, devoid of any comfortable mattresses, to maintain a state of constant alertness. I had even forgotten what it was like to sit in a chair. Months had passed and I had not eaten a square meal or slept on a bed. My hut was rundown, tucked away in the woods, far from civilization. The chilly winds would run through my bones like water through a sponge. There was no electricity, no flushing toilet and no running water. It was an ancient environment, the kind that the great *rishis* lived in once.

Completely disconnected from the outside world, with no human contact, I observed strict silence and solitude. I had given up on everything I possibly could, except just my own life, and yet there was no light. I didn't think that the forces of nature were testing me. Instead, I felt they were humiliating me. Yes, I felt humiliated because foregoing all reason and sense, I had left everything behind to pursue my calling. Maybe, I had dialled the wrong number or maybe my calling was a hoax.

And, I didn't know what was more humiliating – to give up my years of pursuit with an admission that I had blindly devoted and wasted my life for a cause that amounted to nothing or to continue my *sadhana* without knowing if there was any truth to it at all. But, I did know one thing: if I had any chance at discovering my own truth, it would not come by quitting.

With a view to persist, once again, I would wipe my tears and renew my resolve and resume my meditation with great determination and faith. That does not mean though that my path somehow became easier just because by vowing to not give up. On the contrary, the firmer I resolved, the louder became the voice of the inner critic. I had faith alright, but I also had a sceptical mind that was ever eager to reason.

My questioning mind wasn't a challenge, my doubting mind was. Each one of us has two minds, you know. Our positive mind is like the beautiful musk deer. It runs through the jungle of emotions and thoughts spreading fragrance. It is swift, agile, and confident and it doesn't collide. It carves its own path. So is our negative mind, unfortunately, which is like an ugly cockroach with two irritating antennas of self-doubt and negativity. It walks through our delicious food of hope, our clean home of dreams. It breeds rapidly. It reminds you constantly that you don't have it in you or that you don't deserve it.

You build castles of hope and dreams, but one wave of self-doubt or one pounding of guilt and it turns into a dike of dune, almost indistinguishable from the rest of the beach. And you start to see yourself as just a tiny particle of sand, of dust, like everyone else in the world, on the beach. You begin to think that you have nothing special in you, that you can't possibly be the castle or live in one.

The path of *sadhana* for me was not much dissimilar. On some days I would feel that I was progressing but just the next day it would all feel pointless. One day I would think of myself as a great yogi who could put up with the unforgiving Himalayan weather, who could practice extreme austerities, someone who lived unafraid among the wild animals, a yogi who slept on the floor among rats and rodents, among scorpions and snakes. The next day, I would feel like an absolute dunce, a victim of ridicule, who gave up his life of comforts and lived away from civilization like an unlettered caveman.

"What are you trying to do? What are you hoping to accomplish? Do you really think you can awaken kundalini in this day and age? Do you think that God will show up in person? You crack me up, you do. I can't believe you, with all your education and exposure, you believe in this nonsense." My mind often barged into my *sadhana* with such questions and statements. It would try to shake my faith and demean me. It even succeeded, but only temporarily and occasionally.

Gradually, I learned that this was just noise. It was the blabbering of my mind that was not dependent on what I did or didn't. Like a demented ally, it would keep on rambling and the only way to shut it down was to not pay attention to it. I learned to not battle my scepticism but to ignore it. By shifting my attention, I figured a way to keep my consciousness yoked to my object of meditation. I chose faith over self-doubt. I picked discipline over procrastination. I settled for hope over despair. I kept meditating like the Ganges – ceaseless and flowing.

Meanwhile, monsoons had come and gone. Many lush green mountains were looking bit sparse at the advent of fall. Dryness and extreme cold was setting in. Days had become extremely short. Winters had announced their arrival. It would snow on most days. But, eventually, like all seasons, those days passed as well. Sun was taking a longer stroll on its path from east to west, days were becoming sunnier again. Beautiful red, white and mauve flowers bedecked solemn trees. Tiny flowers covered a large area of the ground. New leaves were adorning old trees now.

Nature looked like a bride dressed up for the most important moment of her life. Squirrels, snakes, deer, boars, bear, langurs, mongoose, weasels, rabbits and badgers were out. It looked like one grand celebration. Spring had arrived. Yet my own heart was barren like a winter garden covered with snow – cold and white. There was no harmony, no melody and no rhythm in my existence. I was still a struggling meditator. Clinging to my exhausting routine, I was still meditating with all the fervour and courage I could muster.

Spring too ended its sojourn and went back into the mysterious lap of Mother Divine and it was raining again. Everything in nature had either grown, evolved or moved on. Everything and everyone, except me. I was still where I had begun – clueless. There were occasional experiences and visions but nothing that was consistent and persistent.

By then, I had experienced extraordinary and deep sensations on all my chakras and in *sahasrara*, but they would disappear as soon as I would finish my session of meditation. This wasn't acceptable to me. It was like you work very hard to earn a million dollars but you can only spend them as long as you are in the bank. The moment you walk out of the building, your wealth is lost and your account balance goes back to zero.

I was dying to experience that state of superconscious-ness, that supranormal awareness where you feel oneness with everything around you, that supreme union that stays with you forever. This was eternal bliss for true *samadhi* in my view. This was my spiritual wealth, my Goddess, awakening of the kundalini. I had let go off the temporary material world to experience this permanent bliss and if even this was a temporary feeling, I'd might as well smoke pot and feel good.

Other than the fleeting experiences and intermittent sensations, although very deep, there was nothing else to bank on.

Until one day.

On the thatched roof of my hut covered by tarpaulin, raindrops were constantly falling like thoughts in a restless mind. These beads of pristine Himalayan water would bounce on the roof and then, mingling with each other, they would simply merge and become water. Some of this water would leak through the cracks and keep collecting just a few inches from where I sat, motionless, in deep absorption, but aware.

This day's awareness was different; the type I had never experienced before. I could hear every single raindrop that fell on the roof. I could almost feel when it united with another drop. I could sense them merging and becoming tiny brooks before they would seep through the cracks and gaps and make puddles in my hut. With my eyes still closed, I shifted my attention to the inside of my hut. I could no longer hear the rain, which was particularly deafening because of the drops falling on the tarp.

Instead, I heard a spider crawling on one of the walls. I could sense its thin legs move cautiously. Every single one of its eight hairy legs as if had tiny sensors because they moved in perfect synchronization. Even its legs were sensing the surroundings as if they had a brain of their own. I could hear the spider move about its tiny appendages (pedipalps) in the air to sense any danger before it would make the next step. My mind's eye was seeing it as clearly as my external eye would see a giant mountain in the broad daylight. I could feel every movement of the spider. Just then a doubt crept in. Was I just imagining it or it was actually happening?

In a rare move, I chose to open my eyes and cast a glance in the direction of the spider. There it was, moving exactly as I had seen it. I shifted my attention outside and once again the rain was as audible as before, as if every single raindrop marked its presence like children do in classrooms.

In this all pervading awareness, you experience a union that is beyond words. I wasn't just hearing everything around me, I was feeling it. The same energy that makes water move and makes you move too. The same life force that makes a spider's heart beat and makes your heart beat too. This is the common thread, the unbroken flow of energy, on which pearls of universal existence are strewn.

Other dimensions of existence and awareness were opening gently like petals of lotus do upon sunrise. Roughly seventy-five million light years away I became aware of the existence of a planet, two and half times the size of earth, green, with water and supportive of life-forms. I saw another one, much closer, about 500 light years away. Several months later, when I descended from the Himalayas, it turned out that NASA had indeed confirmed the candidature of a planet called Kepler-22 about 600 light years away from earth. I wasn't surprised. Those deep sensations, that awakening, had become a permanent state of my mind.

The boat of my life was sailing freely now in the vast ocean of bliss and equanimity. I felt this newfound bliss while walking, talking, eating, thinking, sitting, while doing any act. I was my own bank now, my wealth lived within me. I came to the realization that kundalini is indeed real and its awakening is nothing short of the realization of the goddess.

As you walk the path of awakening, you begin to see how everything in our universe is interdependent and interconnected, with no exceptions. Your consciousness and your circle of insight start and continue to expand. Just like the slightest movement of the tiny spider entered into my sphere of consciousness, you start to realize how even the tiniest of action performed even millions of miles away has an impact on you, and vice-versa.

This insight is the seed of liberation. You no longer see yourself as a separate entity who's struggling for existence. This is an utterly liberating feeling and leads to a near permanent kind of profound peace and absorption.

What's even more beautiful is that anyone who is willing to put in the effort can experience it.

In a nutshell: if you do what I did, you'll get what I got. This is the simple science of *sadhana*. Let me show you where to begin the actual practice.

THE LOCATION OF CHAKRAS

The *sadhana* of kundalini starts with first correctly identifying the location of chakras on your body. The six chakras and the seventh *sahasrara* are in a straight line and their distance from each other can vary by a few centimeters depending on the height, structure and constitution of your body. It is important to pinpoint the location of chakras as accurately as possible. Doing so, greatly increases your chances of success because when you meditate at the correct spot, deep sensations start to manifest within six months.

Here is how to identify the location of chakras in your body. Use your right hand if you are right-handed and left hand if you are left-handed.

1. Place the little finger of your hand on the navel. Your navel is the solar plexus or the *manipura* chakra.

2. Stretch your hand fully upwards and see where the tip of the thumb touches. This is your heart plexus or the *anahata* chakra.

3. Place your little finger exactly where your thumb

touched on the heart plexus and stretch your hand fully once again to see where the thumb touches now. This is your throat plexus or the *vishuddhi* chakra.

4. Once again, put your little finger exactly where your thumb was and move one full hand-measure up. Your thumb is now touching your brow plexus or the *agya* chakra.

5. Place your little finger where you just found your brow chakra and stretch your hand fully again. Your thumb will be now touching your crown chakra or *Sahasrara*.

6. Go back to the navel. Put your thumb on your navel, stretch your hand and go one full hand measure down. Your little finger is now touching your sacral plexus or *svadhishthana* chakra.

7. Place your thumb where your little finger just was and stretch your hand fully downwards one more time. Your little finger is now touching your root plexus or *muladhara* chakra.

Make sure to take your hand measure from the tip of your little finger to the tip of your thumb. Just like if you stretch your arms, the distance from the tip of one middle finger to the other is same as the height of your body, the distance between one chakra and the other is exactly one hand. Only your hand can accurately pinpoint the location of your chakras.

FIVE ELEMENTS OF CHAKRA MEDITATION

From this point on, we'll be deviating from what all you may have read till date about chakras in other texts. In true chakra meditation, the number of petals, the associative deity, and the various letters on each petal have no role. The quality, intensity and duration of concentration are the only real factors. Anything that helps you attain superior concentration will help you in kundalini awakening.

If you practice yoga *asanas* (postures), *bandhas* (locks) and mudras (gestures), you are free to continue them. They are for your body fitness and they will improve your ability to sit still for longer periods of time.

If you practice *pranayama*, breath regulation, or any other exercises, you can continue them. All these are auxiliary practices and they help you in your meditation. Their contribution or importance is minimal though when it comes to chakra meditation.

For each chakra, there are five important elements that affect your chances of success:

1. Visualization

In each chapter on chakras, I've specified the color of each chakra. This is the only visualization that matters. There is absolutely no need to confuse yourself with attendant deities and numerous implements they are holding. Trying to count the number of petals and meditating on them only dilutes your focus. The simpler is the visualization, the more effective is your meditation. For each chakra simply visualize its color at the location of that chakra.

2. Mantra

The sacred syllable of each chakra is a potent seed of energy. Once you reach an intermediate stage, you'll realize that each chakra actually resonates with the sound of its seed syllable. The most important thing to remember is that you can't do visualization and mantra at the same time. You will have to divide your time between visualization and mantra meditation of each chakra.

As you build the intensity of your practice, meditate on the visualization as much as you can and when you get tired of visualization turn to mantra meditation for that chakra. The goal is to build your concentration on the chakra while retaining lucidity and awareness of the mind.

3. Posture

I cannot overstate the importance of correct posture. There are ten vital energies in your body that affects everything you think, speak and do. Correct posture helps you in channeling these energies so they pave the way for the awakening of the most potent of all energies – the kundalini.

Ideally, you should be sitting cross-legged but if you can't sit cross-legged then sit comfortably in a chair. At any rate, your back should be straight like an arrow. Your neck slightly, just barely, bent and your hands resting in your lap.

During your meditation, you must be still like a rock. The more stillness you gain of the mind, the more stillness comes in your body naturally. The reverse is also true. Stillness of the body is an unfailing sign of an advanced yogi. Unnecessary and energy wasting movements like shaking your legs or being fidgety etc go away on their own as stability begins to take shape in the mind.

4. Concentration

If you practice the first three, your single-pointed concentration will improve on its own. No awakening of the kundalini is possible without building your concentration. For that matter, no success in any meditation is possible without superior concentration. It is for this reason that even Patanjali puts concentration before even meditation. Concentration is not meditation.

In fact, good concentration leads to good meditation. Concentration is the act of building focus and meditation is the art of retaining it without losing awareness. Success in piercing of chakras depends on the quality of your meditation. The better the quality of your one-pointed concentration, the quicker and longer-lasting are the results.

5. Diet regulation

It is important to consume diet according to the chakra you are meditating on. Go through various chakras like rungs of a ladder and regulate your diet in line with the chakra you are meditating on. In each chapter on the chakras, I've specified foods that are suitable for each chakra.

In any case, avoid spicy, oily and deep-fried foods. Being a vegetarian will greatly help your cause because vegetarian food infuses you with *sattvic* energy.

HOW TO MEDITATE ON CHAKRAS

For a determined and sincere practitioner, piercing the first two chakras, that is, root and sacral plexus, requires a devoted practice of one year each. Subsequent chakras need roughly six months each. This is assuming that you are able to devote an average of two hours every day, each day of the year. Those two hours should be split into two sessions of one hour each or three sessions of forty minutes each.

Your first reaction may be that you are very busy and that you can't find two hours every day. You may start with less but the truth is real results only come from intense meditation. And intense meditation requires unwavering commitment. Let's not forget that the awakening of kundalini is one of the most rewarding and difficult meditations.

We study in school for six hours every day and do so for more than fifteen years before graduating with a basic degree that doesn't even guarantee a job. While in a job, we work an average of eight to ten hours to earn a basic salary at the end of the month. We only get two or three weeks of vacation in one year. A concert pianist invests an average of ten thousand hours in practice before attaining proficiency. Not to mention that all artists or musicians continue to practice throughout their lives.

In much the same manner, awakening of kundalini requires practice, effort, time and commitment. It is not just a feel-good meditation; here you are talking about an extraordinary transformation of the self. You are not just aiming to create but you are going straight to the source of the creation. Think of kundalini *sadhana* as learning the piano or performing in the Olympics – if you want to stand a chance at winning, you have to put in the efforts.

My own experience has been that if you devote roughly seven hours every day in quality chakra meditation, you will have your first significant experience within six months. In other words, if you can meditate on chakras as a full-time job, you will have the first major promotion within six months. During the peak of my practice, I meditated an average of twenty-two hours on a daily basis.

When you reach a certain degree of intensity, your hunger, sleep, habits, mind and thought processes undergo a significant and irreversible transformation.

As a persistent meditator, it's important to meditate on one chakra at a time. Move to the next chakra once you have championed the first one. How to know if you are ready to meditate on the next chakra? Once you have meditated on one chakra for a minimum period of six months (one year in the case of root and sacral plexus) and you experience deep sensations every time you meditate on the chakra, you are ready to go to the next one. How quickly you get to the next stage depends on how intense an effort you put in.

For all practical purposes, let's assume that you will meditate for only two hours every day. This is how your session can look like:

1. Five minutes of deep breathing to normalize your breath.

2. Ten minutes of meditation on the brow chakra to normalize your energies.

3. Forty minutes of meditation on the chakra of your primary focus.

4. Five minutes of deep breathing again to relax your body.

With respect to the third point, if you feel tired during those forty minutes, then you can alternate between visualizing the color of the chakra and meditating on its seed syllable. As you progress on the path, gradually, you could maintain a sort of meditative awareness all the time. While bathing, driving, eating etc you could simply meditate with mindfulness. This creates a rhythm in the mind. Noise becomes music then.

Meditate for only six days every week, taking a break of one day. A good break refreshes your mind. Try to start your meditation the same time every day. During chakra meditation, if you can avoid alcohol or other intoxicating substances, it will be so much better. This is because while in the short-term while they may actually help you to meditate better, they are depressants and will impair your ability to visualize and concentrate well in a medium to longer term.

⚕

A devoted disciple learned meditation from his master. No matter how hard he tried, he just couldn't focus in the beginning. However, one day he experienced deep absorption during his meditation.

"Guruji," he said joyously, "today my meditation was most amazing."

"Don't worry," the guru replied in a matter-of-fact tone, "this will pass. Just stay course."

"But, I think I have it figured now."

"This feeling too will pass," the master said and went about his business.

The disciple thought it was strange that his guru neither encouraged him nor appreciated his progress. His meditation went really well for another few days and just when he thought he was actually progressing, he started feeling restless and distracted again. The harder he tried the worse his meditation got.

Greatly dismayed, he approached his guru again.

"Guruji," he said disheartened, "I've not been able to meditate at all. I just can't focus."

"Don't worry," the master said softly, "this will pass. Just stay on course."

"But, I think I've lost it completely."

"This feeling too will pass," the guru replied. "Keep meditating."

⚚

When you embark on the path of kundalini awakening, on some days you may feel great sensations, you may feel that you have already made remarkable progress. Don't let it illude you. If before devoting the required time, you feel that you are ready to meditate on the next chakra, almost always you'll be wrong. It is absolutely necessary to develop consistency in the quality of your concentration.

On some days, you'll feel that you just can't meditate, that this whole meditation and all is not for you. Don't lose heart. Just meditate a bit more. Don't give up. No one has ever learned anything by giving up. Continue to meditate with resolve and awareness and the kundalini will pierce the chakra. There is no other way.

Start from the root chakra and keep progressing one step at a time. Every time you reach a milestone, you'll unlock a divine aspect that you didn't even know existed in you. This gradual transformation shapes you into a new person, into a better person as you continue to discover new things about yourself.

You may wonder if you can use the newly found energies from chakras to have better relationships, jobs, performance, mood and so forth? The answer is yes. It doesn't mean if you don't know how to speak Chinese, you will start speaking it. It simply means that gaining a remarkable cohesiveness, the purity of your thought and the clarity in your mind will help you attain your goals faster than any other approach.

With each step you make on the path of kundalini *sadhana*, you unlock a new level of your consciousness. The clarity of your thought begins to improve noticeably. Your memory improves and an inexplicable stillness arises in the body. You feel more grounded, you find it hard to react to other's criticism, and you begin to maintain an awareness without being affected about what is going on around you. You start to see that your thoughts have started manifesting in real life, they begin to materialize.

You are able to attract your desired objects with greater ease. Your sense of individuality starts to find its place in your life, lifestyle and living. You and everyone around you notice a definitive positive change in you. Your imperfections no longer are like the thumb in front of your eye blocking your vision of the bright sun or the glorious moon, instead, they become like the temporary clouds that dissipate on their own. Even your imperfections, like the tiny and twinkling stars add beauty to the universe of your existence.

MASTER THE SEVEN
CHAKRAS

THE ROOT PLEXUS

MULADHARA CHAKRA

Kundalini, after having drunk the nectar from *sahasrara*, the thousand-petal lotus, has fallen to the grossest level; that is the root chakra. At the base of your spine, it's called *muladhara* chakra. Awakening of the kundalini starts with piercing of this chakra.

"*mūlādhārāmbujārūḍhā*
pañcavaktrā'sthisaṃsthitā,
aṅkuśādipraharaṇā varadādiniṣevitā.
mudgaudanāsaktacittā sākinyambāsvarūpiṇī."
(*Lalita Sahasranama*, 106)

THE LITERAL MEANING

Based in the root chakra is the devi with five faces. This devi is also situated in the bones. She holds a goad and a benedictory hand gesture. She loves food prepared with lentils and her name is Sakini.

THE ESOTERIC MEANING

The five-faced devi is not an actual form with five faces. Instead, it refers to the most important aspects of your life, your body and your living. We have five conative organs with which you perform actions. These organs are: hands, two feet, mouth, genitals and anus. We have five cognitive organs or sensory organs, as they are called. These cognitive organs are: eye, ear, nose, tongue, and skin. We are made up of five elements namely, earth, water, fire, air and space. These are gross elements. They have physical existence and are visible to the naked eye.

Gross elements represent the lowest plane of existence. Even the animals have all of the above. So, what makes us different to animals? Intellect and intelligence. We have the kind of intelligence that animals don't have. We can improve ourselves thereby enriching the society and the world at large.

The energy in this chakra does not only reside there. In the verse above, the next word is *asthi-samsthita*, it's situated in your bones too. And here is the real hidden meaning. Meditating on the *muladhara* chakra improves the health of your bones.

Devi in this chakra is holding an *ankush*, a goad. A goad is a pointed implement that is used to control elephants generally. I once saw a mahout control a rogue elephant rather effortlessly. He simply put the hook on its large ear and used the spike at its neck. Immediately the elephant sat down. Since *muladhara* is one of the first chakras to meditate on, your challenge to stay focused will be as big as an elephant; it will almost be like taming the elephant. You don't need to feel frustrated or fight with it, for it'll run over you. You simply need to use the goad of mindfulness and determination and carry on.

Universe always makes way for the one who is positive and determined. If you don't give up, all obstacles give in. Hence, the devi is holding one hand in benediction.

Devi likes *mudgaudana*, soup of beans and rice. *Mudga* specifically refers to the lentils known as black gram or black lentil (Latin: *Phaseolus mungo* or *Vigna mungo*). There is a hidden meaning too in this disclosure: during the six months you meditate on the root chakra, you should regulate your diet so it has more beans and rice. Avoid fatty foods as they set you back in *sadhana* by making you lethargic. A spoon of butter or ghee is okay but no fried foods.

Mastery over the *muladhara* chakra bestows upon you fine health. Notably it is good for the bones. You develop greater sensitivity to the five subtle elements of sound, touch, taste, form and smell. One of the first signs of mastery of the *muladhara* chakra is a healthy decrease in appetite; lesser quantities start to suffice you because you now process all the gross elements much better than you ever did before.

With heightened senses, you experience everything with greater intensity and you develop a certain degree of sensitivity towards all sentient being – the hallmark of a true spiritual person.

With prolonged meditation on the *muladhara* chakra, you begin to feel lighter. The weight of carnal desires and gross thoughts start to diffuse and give way to a feeling of well-being and peace.

The scripture is quiet about the color of this chakra but the source from where I got this *sadhana* isn't. The color of this chakra is orange, vibrant orange. Devi's name is Sakini and therefore, the seed syllable of this chakra becomes SAM (pronounced more like 'sung' with a soft 'g' in the end. Only your guru can disclose the exact pronunciation). I am well aware that the traditional texts state the seed syllable to be LAM for this chakra.

Here, I would like to reiterate that the secrets of *sadhana* are never to be found in books. Ultimately, more than the syllables, it's the quality of visualization that makes all the difference.

THE SACRAL PLEXUS

SVADHISHTHANA CHAKRA

At the point of your genitals is the sacral plexus, *svadhishthana* chakra, the original abode of Kundalini.

> "svādhiṣṭhānāmbujagatā caturvaktramanoharā,
> śūlādyāyudhasampannā pītavarṇā'tigarvitā.
> medoniṣṭhā madhuprītā bandhinyādisamanvitā,
> dadhyannāsaktahṛdayā kākinīrūpadhāriṇī."
>   (Lalita Sahasranama, 104-105)

THE LITERAL MEANING

The devi in *svadishthana* chakra has four faces. She's of yellow color and is holding a spike. She is situated in the body fat, likes honey and is surrounded by Bandhinya and other attendant energies. The devi likes victuals with yogurt and her name is Kakini

THE ESOTERIC MEANING

From an ant to an elephant, anything with consciousness has two things in common without fail – the desire to live and the desire to copulate. In fact, it's unfair to call them desires. They are not desires but two core principles of evolution, of nature. This is how nature has grown, this is how species have evolved and progressed. There is a natural attachment, a clinging to life that comes from our desire to live. We want to live forever and we want to be happy in our life and pursuits.

To feel that happiness, we constantly cling to everything we build or acquire. We don't want to lose our wealth or our loved ones. We don't want any suffering. But no growth is possible without letting go. Whatever we wish to attain, we have to give up something in return. We give up our childhood to be youthful. We sacrifice our time to attain our goals. The more we are able to let go, the more we are able to accomplish. And, this leads to the second desire.

The desire to copulate, the need for a sexual union at its core is the most liberating emotion. A man and a woman remove their coverings; they bare themselves to each other. There is no pretense, no artificiality. In that moment of climax, there is no ego, there is no clinging. It's all about letting go. Even though they are united physically and emotionally, both the partners have surrendered to each other to experience one of the most divine pleasures – orgasm.

It is not possible to reach an orgasm if you have inhibitions, if you have fears. And no matter how much you resist or hold back, nature propels each living entity towards a sexual union. Out of our ego and conditioned beliefs, we may label it as good or bad, sacred or sacrilegious, but nature knows that it is only in letting go that you experience the greatest liberation, that you grow and help nature grow.

'Sva' means self and 'adhisthana' means place. Svadhisthana or the sacral plexus refers to the normal, natural abode of kundalini. This chakra is located at the point of genitals. It is from here that we express our sexual energy, procreate and derive the pleasure of sex.

Kundalini, however, has descended to the lowest chakra because it has drunk the nectar from sahasrara, the thousand petal lotus in our brain. No pleasure, not even sexual pleasure, can be experienced in the absence of a brain. It instructs, drives, controls and experiences all pleasures. Therefore, both our brain and our sacral energy must in be harmony to experience any sexual pleasure. A person who is brain dead can't be aroused, for example.

The need for sexual pleasure is so innate and great in each individual that while it is our creative fluid, it is often also the cause of our great downfall. It makes us cling to our partner. We want a sort of exclusivity; we want to own them and mould them the way it suits us. In that desire for exclusivity, emotions of jealousy, hatred and envy arise. We lose control of ourselves. The good in us gets covered like clouds cover sun.

Classical texts state that because kundalini drank the nectar from the sahasrara chakra, it lost control of itself and went down all the way to muladhara, even slipping down from its own place. *Muladhara* also means the root foundation, the absolute basis. This represents the reality of our world where having sex is simply a matter of slaking lust for most people. Forgetting the potency of this creative power, our modern society has mostly reduced this union to a mere act where more and more people are looking outside their relationships for more sex. We no longer look upon harnessing this creative energy to experience a union at all levels – physical, emotional and spiritual. Instead, most of us around are just happy with just the physical aspect; they are happy to come and go, if you see what I mean.

They are not to be blamed though, because they have not yet experienced the complete union, a meeting of the bodies, minds and souls, altogether at the same level. It is not taught in any school. Sex is a private act, oneness isn't. It's a cosmic dimension.

This is where kundalini and the sacral plexus come into play. *Lalita Sahasranama* states that there is a four-faced devi who presides over this chakra. In reality, this devi represents four aspects of sexuality and four aspects of the human mind.

FOUR ASPECTS OF SEXUALITY

Sex is not just a physical act. In fact, most of the sexual pleasure is a cerebral act – it occurs in the brain. Whether sex is in the mind, in words or in actual physicality, not everyone does it the same way. The manner in which you perform a sexual union and the subsequent fulfillment you derive from sex depends upon where you are on the spiritual ladder.

Tantric texts, such as *Nitya Tantra*, *Kubjika Tantra*, *Kularnava Tantra*, *Mahanirvana Tantra*, categorize all men into three segments based on their temperaments. They are: *divya* (divine), *vira* (valiant) and *pashu* (animal). However, when it comes to sexuality, there is a fourth temperament too, called *manushya bhava* (human sentiment). Any sexual act is generally performed in one of these four tendencies of divine, warrior, human or animal.

The Animal Way

From the Sanskrit word '*paash*', which means chain or fetter, comes the word *pashu*, an animal. The one who is chained to any habit, thought or desire is a *pashu*. For an animal, sex is not an emotional need but a base carnal desire, a pure biological need. A man who enjoys sexual union in the *pashu bhava* will be rough and violent in his act.

The animal way does not concern with the feelings of the partner. It is simply a matter of satiating their lust. To a man (or a woman) in the animal sentiment, they can sleep just about with anyone. They don't have to be in love, they don't need to feel love. Just like a dog will happily take a piece of bread from anyone, a sexual animal is only looking for a piece of flesh.

They will extinguish themselves as ably in a brothel as much as with their partner. The basis of this relationship is only sexual gratification. Animals simply look for an avenue to allay their sexual thirst; they can drink from any pond. A human being with similar tendencies is the equivalent of *pashu*. He or she just has to get to the climax regardless of who the partner is. And in doing so, he won't mind hurting the other person – physically or emotionally.

The Human Way

The word *manushya* means one who takes *ashya* (refuge) in manas (mind or heart). A step above from *pashu* is the *manushya bhava*, the human sentiment. While animals too show emotions, we are a lot more evolved and complex. In the human way, you need to feel love for the other person and you need to feel loved back before you can entertain the thought of sleeping with them.

How fulfilled you feel depends on a myriad of feelings and sentiments including love, bonding, attachment and a sense of belonging. You don't look upon the other person as an outlet for your lust. Instead, you wish to love them and be with them. You want to make a difference to his or her life and in return. You yearn for their attention. You wish to be loved back, you crave for reciprocation. This gives you a sense of belonging and attachment. You want to be everything to them and vice-versa too.

Our animal instincts are so innate in us that for the majority out there, it's hard to love in *manushya bhava* alone. Most of us alternate between the animal way and the human way. At times, when animal instincts take over, one can be very rough during an intercourse. Just like animals look upon a mating partner in heat, most men can simply evaluate another woman lasciviously without feeling an ounce of love for her.

No matter how many people we sleep with, we are not animals after all. We are humans, and therefore, we can never feel that sense of completeness and fulfillment with physical intimacy alone. Somewhere, our emotional and spiritual thirst is far greater than our sexual appetite because we are spiritual beings. Hence, when we rise above our animalistic tendencies, we look upon and require sex in the human way.

In such a state of mind, in *manushya bhava*, sexual union quenches our emotional and sentimental thirst too. It fulfills our great and deep seated desire for companionship and togetherness.

The Warrior Way

Vira bhava is the sentiment of a warrior. In *Rudrayamalam*, *vira* is defined as a tantric adept who is just one step below *divya bhava*, divinity. In *Rig Veda*, a *vira* is a term given to progeny. The one who can subdue enemies is a *vira* but above all, the one who harnesses his creative fluid (*virya*) is *vira*.

Creative fluid is referred to the reproductive fluid in both men and women, the fluid that make men virile and women fertile. In *vira bhava*, one of the two partners is always dominant. Sexual union in this *bhava* serves a twofold purpose. First, the dominant partner feels a sense of victory. Like a warrior, the more they are in control, the more gratifying it is for them. Second, they feel elated by winning over their partner with a display of their physical strength and endurance.

Unlike the human way, a warrior has a greater sense of detachment. For him, sexual union is a part of life, an aspect of their *sadhana*. Just like a warrior feels protective about his king, the one in *vira bhava* feels protective about their partner. This sense of protection should not be confused for possessiveness. A warrior protects out of a sense of duty and not attachment.

An animal's sexual union lasts no more than a few tens of seconds. A human's may last for a few minutes, but the one in *vira bhava* gains satisfaction only by prolonging the duration of their physical union. Unlike the animal way, *vira bhava* is not just about satiating lust, and unlike the human way, it is not out of some deep urge for belongingness. *Vira bhava* is about being there for the other person as their strength and support. It is about being the one they can rely on for security.

The final stage in sexual consciousness is the divine way. Animal wants to slake, human wants to possess, warrior wants to protect, but divine sets everything free.

The Divine Way

Krishna would sit by the banks of the midnight-blue river, Yamuna. With moonbeams gently falling on his serene countenance, on the trees, on the river, everything would be softly lit like love. Love is a soft emotion, a gentle expression. He would start playing his flute. The divine blow from his pure lips would make a hollow flute sound most mellifluous. The music of life would come alive and love would dance to its tune sending all *gopis* into a trance.

Leaving their homes, husbands, children, cattle and belongings behind, they would come running to Krishna. Whatever they were doing, they would simply drop it and follow the hypnotic sound of the flute. They wanted to give everything they had to Krishna. The *gopis* would anoint him with sandalwood paste, some would garland him with fresh flowers and offer him betel leaves. Some *gopis* would press his legs while some other would gently comb his hair. They would admire his flute for Krishna always kept it close, for he would touch his flute with his lips. They asked the flute that what good karma it did that it got to be Krishna's flute.

"I emptied myself," said the flute. "I do not retain anything, I don't cling. I've surrendered completely and I simply allow myself to be played whenever he wishes. I never speak, only he speaks through me."

The *gopis*, like the flute, had completely surrendered to Krishna's will. There was no jealousy, no envy among each other. There was no clinging because they were there to serve Krishna and not to own him. It was not the *pashu* (slaking lust), *manushya* (possessiveness) or the *vira bhava* (protective), it was the *divya bhava* (freedom).

Divya bhava, the divine temperament, is the ultimate stage in the evolution of sexual consciousness. For the one operating in *divya bhava* engaging in a sexual act is only an extension, an expression of love. This *bhava* was exemplified by Krishna with the *gopis*.

As you progress on the path of awakening of the kundalini, you learn to channelize your sexual energy. You become a giver. You have no demands and your joy only comes from giving all your love and joy to the other person. You offer your body, mind and soul in *divya bhava*. A sexual union is not to gratify any personal urges but to unite in love at all levels.

Only three types of people experience *divya bhava* in a sexual union. First is the completely selfless person who is simply playing the role of a giver with utmost compassion and care. Such a person, when making love, is only concerned about making his or her partner complete. Their own gratification and joy comes from giving love and security to the other person. Like Krishna, his love is the purest, devoid of any attachments.

Second is someone who has totally surrendered in love. This person no longer has any personal preferences, there is no personal agenda. He or she has placed the other person on the altar of their heart. This person is in a sexual union because they want to completely offer absolutely every ounce of whatever they have. Like *gopis*, they want to serve and be the strength of the other person. Once *gopis* took Krishna to be their divine lover, they surrendered unconditionally. This surrender is a sublime form of bhakti.

The third type of person who can make love in a *divya bhava* is a tantric adept. Completely detached and with no desire to prolong the sexual union, a yogi wants to fill his consort with divine energy so she may experience a deep sense of oneness even long after the sexual embrace. It's a spiritual hangover. Shiva unites with Shakti in this *divya bhava*.

In *divya bhava*, the boundaries between male and female blur before disappearing completely. It doesn't feel like you are making love to another person. Instead, it feels that you are with your own extension, your mirror-self, your counterpart. A man is exploring his own feminine side in a woman and a woman is exploring her own masculine aspect, the right brain is getting in touch with the left brain, creativity is gaining oneness with logic. It is mind looking at itself.

The four-faced devi in the sacral plexus also refers to the four aspects of the mind. A lot happens in our mind from the moment a thought emerges to the time we actually act on it. No matter how impulsive an action is, it invariably goes through four phases. These four phases are the four aspects of our mind.

THE FOUR ASPECTS OF MIND

The four aspects of the human mind are collectively referred to as the *chatush-anatahkarana*, the four seats of thoughts and feelings. They are: manas (mind), *buddhi* (intelligence), *citta* (consciousness), *ahamakara* (conception of one's individuality).

Any desire or thought first springs in our mind. If we don't do anything about it the thought ends right there. This is the lifespan of a thought. But, if we are unable to let go of that thought, it is passed onto our consciousness. We start to deliberate and cogitate on the thought, reflecting on its pros and cons, its benefits and costs. Consciousness, though, can't make a decision on its own. Once we are done with the deliberation, the thought is passed onto the third aspect of our mind, that is, intelligence.

Intelligence makes the final decision whether we are going to pursue our thoughts or not. If we decide to turn our thought into our reality, it gets passed onto the ego, our sense of individual existence. Our ego drives us to create and guard our individuality. It stops us from experiencing the divine union because ego is always insecure. It separates us from what's around us. Ego wants control and charge, it is scared of surrendering. When we get hurt by anyone's actions, it is our ego that gets hurt. Sexual union is one of the most gratifying feelings because it requires that you completely drop your ego.

Your sexuality, sexual conduct and sexual thoughts, all of which can be controlled by meditating on the *svadishthana* chakra, have a direct and immediate impact on your state of mind and consciousness.

The devi holding a spike encourages the seeker to build

one-pointed concentration on this chakra. Bandhini and other attendant devis refer to the *bandhas*, locks, practiced in yoga to augment your practice of meditation on chakras. *Bandhas* are not required and personally, I don't do them. I have always focused on pure meditation.

This devi is established in body fat and likes honey and food with yogurt. It means while practicing meditation on this chakra, you should regulate your diet to include more honey and yogurt. Meditating on this chakra has a positive influence on all physical ailments linked to body fat including problems with cholesterol and blockages in the arteries.

Devi's name of this chakra is Kakini and the seed syllable becomes KAM.

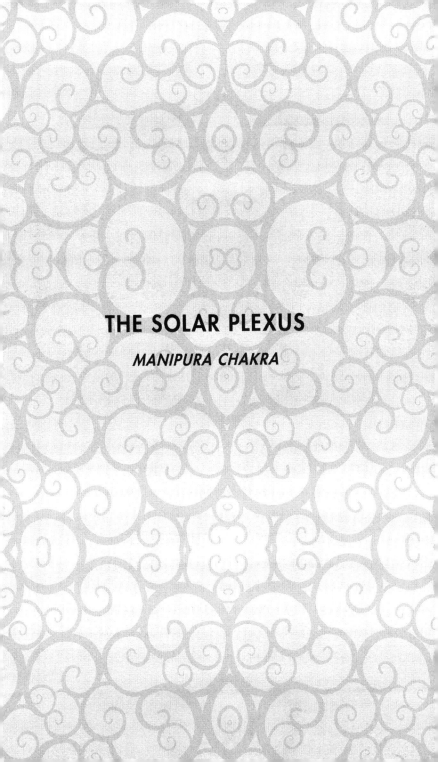

THE SOLAR PLEXUS

MANIPURA CHAKRA

Right on your belly button is the solar plexus, *manipura chakra*.

> "*maṇipūrābjanilayā vadanatrayasaṃyutā,*
> *vajrādikāyudhopetā ḍāmaryādibhirā vṛtā.*
> *raktavarṇā māṃsaniṣṭhā guḍānnaprītamānasā,*
> *samastabhaktasukhadā lākinyambāsvarūpiṇī.*"
>
> (*Lalita Sahasranama*, 102-103)

THE LITERAL MEANING

A three-faced devi is situated in the *manipura* chakra. She is holding a thunderbolt and is surrounded by Damari and other companion energies. She is of red color and situated in your flesh. She loves *guda*, muscovado, (a lump of brown sugar made by boiling sugarcane juice). She grants all forms of comfort to the devotees and assumes of the form of devi Lakini.

THE ESOTERIC MEANING

Manipura chakra is at the point of your navel, the central point of your belly. The three-faced devi refers to the three *doshas* namely, *vata* (wind), *pitta* (bile) and *kapha* (phlegm). Everyone has a natural tendency towards a certain humor. Some are more *vata*, others *pitta* and some *kapha*, while many are mixed. Ayurveda states that the cause of 95 percent of diseases in human body can be traced back to one's stomach. Meditating on the *manipura* chakra appeases the three *doshas*.

The three-faced devi also refers to the three types of food you process. Scriptures classify such foods into *sattvic* (wholesome food packed with goodness), *rajasic* (food that rouses passion) and *tamasic* (food that boosts aggression). Regulation of diet is particularly important when meditating on the navel chakra.

Body heat, one of the most important factors in the physical health, is directly regulated by the *manipura* chakra. Scriptures state that heat first burns food in the stomach, if unregulated, it starts to impact the digestive system and the person suffers from stomach ulcers, liver disorders or constipation. If you don't provide your body with more food to digest and your body suffers from excess heat, then your mouth becomes parched, your lips get chapped and you can suffer from high blood pressure.

The devi is holding a thunderbolt, just like pangs of hunger, you experience sensations in this chakra as if a flash of lightening. Initially, they come and they go. At later stages, they start to settle and you experience constant sensations on the chakra.

The attendant devis refers to the seven auspicious qualities you develop in yourself. The seven devis are Damari, Mangala, Pingala, Dhanya, Bhadrika, Ulka and Siddha; they refer to deep hypnotic voice, good luck, beautiful radiant skin, fine food, noble conduct, light and success respectively.

Interestingly, *manipura* chakra has a deep relationship with intuitive and instinctual faculties of the mind. I have observed on numerous occasions that meditating on *manipura* can sharpen your intuition. The linking of *manipura* chakra with instinct may have its roots in the fact that in the womb you are attached to the umbilical cord from your navel. This is the root of your existence; any learning while you are in the womb, any feed for the body is through your navel. So, your first instincts have a solid connection with your *manipura* chakra.

At par with *agya* chakra (brow plexus), *manipura* is the most important chakra in the awakening of kundalini. As you attain *siddhi* of *manipura*, you are able to regulate your body heat and therefore, maintain better health. Other noticeable effect is the lustre of the skin. A good *sadhaka* emits a soft glow and radiance upon mastery of this chakra. Meditating on the *manipura* chakra also aids in muscular health.

A sincere *sadhaka* who continues to perfect this meditation on his chakra is never disturbed by even long periods of hunger or starvation. He is able to stay up and energetic for long periods even by eating very little.

Stomach is also the seat of your fear. When you are afraid, you first feel it in your belly. Our fears hold us back from reaching our full potential. Mastery of this chakra gives you a sense of calm in uncertain situations in life. A sort of fearlessness arises in you. Those who feel anxious and nervous in conflicts and undesirable situations can benefit much by meditating on the *manipura* chakra.

The devi is situated in the flesh. It means this chakra controls the suppleness of your muscles and any muscular disorders can be corrected by meditating on this chakra. During periods of intense meditation on *manipura*, you should eat more *sattvic* food.

The color of this chakra is red. The name of the devi is Lakini, and, therefore the seed syllable becomes LAM.

THE HEART PLEXUS

ANAHATA CHAKRA

Right in the middle of your chest, a few inches to the right of your heart is the *anahata* chakra.

> *"anāhatābjanilayā śyāmābhā vadanadvayā,*
> *daṃṣṭrojjvalā'kṣamālādidharā rudhirasaṃsthitā.*
> *kālarātryādiśaktyaughavṛtā snigdhaudanapriyā,*
> *mahāvīrendravaradā rākiṇyambāsvarūpiṇī."*
>
> (*Lalita Sahasranama*, 100-101)

THE LITERAL MEANING

Situated in the *anahata* chakra is a two-faced devi of black color. She has bright teeth and is wearing beads of *rudrakasha*. She is present in the blood. She is encircled by attendant devis like Kalaratri and she loves soft and gentle foods cooked with oil. She bestows blessings to the courageous ones and has assumed the form of Rakini.

THE ESOTERIC MEANING

We have two takes on everything in life. This profoundly represents the two aspects of everything – good-bad, right-wrong, true-false; of emotions – positive and negative; and of choices – yes and no. Scriptures call this a duality and it is the seed of all human emotions. You rise above duality and automatically going beyond these temporary states, you reach the shore of eternal peace.

Most of us are totally driven by our feelings. No matter how calm or composed we are, a single surge of anger could get us worked up in no time. In that anger, we spit words like a cobra spits venom. It gives a release to our pent up emotions. We feel good for a little while and then we feel guilty. And then we recall all the things we said that we didn't mean to say. Now feeling of remorse and helplessness takes over. It affects our self-esteem. Emotions of hatred, jealousy, envy, passion, sadness and resentment are no different either. Our emotions are out of control when our actions are not in sync with our thoughts and our feelings. You purify your heart and thoughts purify themselves; actions get aligned on their own then.

The two-faced devi resides in the heart chakra. She represents duality. Living in our world, we are forced to make choices, every day, several times in a day. Our past influences our choices in the present, and our current choices determine the course of our future. The one whose mind and heart are in harmony is naturally more decisive and intuitive. Such a person is able to take decisions and move on. It brings about a sort of fearlessness.

Meditating on the heart chakra affects a profound synchronization between your mind and your heart. As you progress on this chakra, not only you start to experience certain calmness among all the positives and negatives, but you also make a noticeable leap in arriving at decisions. Your talents come to the fore and you are able to stick to your choices with conviction. You are able to see your plans through.

People are mostly indecisive because of two reasons – either they fear the future or they cannot assess the impact of their decision with conviction. A good *sadhaka*, after having gained mastery over *manipura*, can examine their fears without feeling anxious. And with the mastery over this chakra, you gain the ability to take decisions and spring to action.

The devi's bright teeth in the heart chakra indicate that by meditating on this chakra you are able to properly chew on your decisions. You accept both good and undesirable with equal indifference. The devi's teeth are specifically documented as bright, which means that you maintain a brighter, happier disposition among the negatives and the positive life walks you through. You no longer sulk or skulk.

The *akshamala*, beads of *aksh*, do not refer to *rudrakasha* but the fifty letters of the Sanskrit alphabet starting from 'a' and ending with 'ksh'. Any word ever offered to you, pleasant or otherwise, critical or praising, can only be formed from a combination of these fifty letters in the alphabets. If you can remain indifferent to other's opinions by thinking they are merely joining letters from the alphabet and offering you a garland, majority of your reactions will disappear. This can only be done with a certain sense of mindfulness as well as stillness of the energies in the body. When your energies are still, others can't provoke you and if they can't provoke you, you get the time to think through and choose your verbal and mental responses – both internal and external.

The devi is situated in the blood. It means that by meditating on the *anahata* chakra you can correct disorders of the blood.

The devi is surrounded by Kalaratri and four other forms of energies. Their names are Raktadantika, Bhramari, Shakambhari and Durga. However, here Kalaratri refers to a special period of nine nights. This period comes once a year and according to the lunar calendar it starts from the month of *magha* from the sixth day of the waning moon till the night before new moon. The month of *magha* comes in the month of January as per the Gregorian calendar. During these nine nights, meditating on this chakra for four hours during the day and for four hours at night has remarkable results. One should stay on a gluten-free diet during those nine days.

The first thing you notice when you meditate on this chakra is a sense of equanimity. You become more grounded and gain better control over your emotions. When you continue to work towards the *siddhi* of this chakra, various forces of nature start to work with you to help you materialize your dreams. Your ability to take intuitive decisions reaches a whole new level.

The other benefit of meditating on *anahata* chakra is that you experience a certain purification – physical as well as emotional – taking place in you. The quality of your blood improves and you feel more positive. Your impulsive or disagreeable reactions become mellow and mindful.

The practitioner experiences a surge of new courage in his very being. The name of the devi is Rakini. The color is black and the accompanying sound is RAM.

In the traditional texts, the color of the heart chakra is defined as green. For reasons unknown, someone just forcefully connected the seven colors of the rainbow to the seven colors of the chakra. There exists no such real connection in reality. According to *Lalita Sahasranama*, the color of the heart chakra is black.

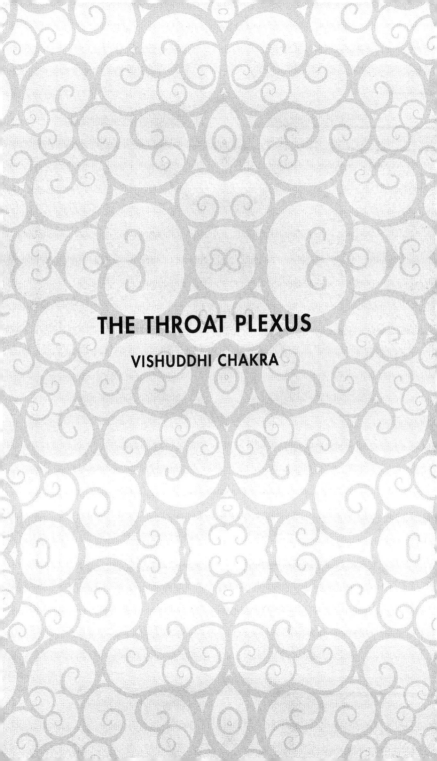

THE THROAT PLEXUS

VISHUDDHI CHAKRA

R ight in the middle of your throat, is *vishuddhi* chakra.

> *"viśuddhicakranilayā"raktavarṇā trilocanā,*
> *khaṭvāṅgādipraharaṇā vadanaikasamanvitā.*
> *pāyasānnapriyā tvaksthā paśulokabhayaṅkarī,*
> *amṛtādimahāśaktisaṃvṛtā ḍākinīśvarī."*
>
> (*Lalita Sahasranama*, 18-19)

THE LITERAL MEANING

A one-faced devi with three eyes is situated in the *vishuddhi* chakra. Her color is that of red sandalwood. She holds the mystical staff and likes food cooked with rice, sugar and milk. She is situated in the skin and creates fright in the animal kingdom. Encircled by Amrita and other devis, her name is Dakini.

THE ESOTERIC MEANING

This is one of the most important chakras. This chakra separates all the lower chakras from the two purest ones that will give birth to incredible insight and extraordinary wisdom in you. *Vishuddha* means completely cleansed and purified. Whenever we drink or eat anything, it sort of becomes sour as soon as it goes below your throat; the food's taste changes. Throat is a transient container. It is not supposed to retain anything, it simply passes on.

The devi is said to have one face because, now you have become the same person inside out now. This is the result of meditating on this chakra. You gain enough inner strength and courage to not wear different faces but simply be absolutely comfortable with who you are, what you are and where you are.

Only in the description of this chakra, references are made to the eyes of the devi. She is called Trilochana, three-eyed. Trilochana is a name used almost exclusively for Shiva, the foremost yogi. Once you master the *Vishuddhi* chakra, only one step remains between the ultimate union of kundalini in *sahasrara*. You are almost Shiva, a true yogi or *yogini* like Him, by the time you finish opening up this chakra.

In one of the puranic legends, Shiva held the most venomous poison in his throat and since then he has been called Nilkantha, the one with blue throat. Some have associated the color blue with the throat chakra. Even though none of this is taught in the inner circles, the books continue to borrow from each other. Less than one percent of seekers show the tenacity and determination to come as far as the throat chakra.

The devi is holding a *khadvanga*, a mystical staff held by Shiva. This is a clear indication that you will undergo major transformation of thought, energy and intelligence by meditating on this chakra. The devi is no longer holding her own implements, but she is holding the ones of Shiva. Here, energy is undergoing a deep transformation – potential energy is transforming into kinetic energy. In the next chakras, the devi is holding no weapons at all. A battle of self transformation will turn into the garden of love, softly lit under the shimmering moon, where Shiva and Shakti, *Purusa* and *Prakriti* will sport in the most divine manner. Efforts will lead to effortlessness; acts will change into phenomena.

The devi likes *payasam*, food cooked with milk, sugar and rice. During the days of intense meditation on this chakra, you should stay on mostly milk in your diet. Your milk diet can include all milk products. Additionally, you can have rice too, and for sugar you can have any fruits that you love. Too much salt, spices, beans, grains and lentils should be avoided.

Meditating on this chakra will give you a radiant skin and will fix disorders of the skin. Ayurvedic texts, notably *Shranagadhar Samhita*, state that skin has seven layers. Meditating on this chakra with the right diet will heal your skin on all the seven levels.

The devi is said to fright the *pasuloka*, the animal kingdom. Meditating on this chakra gives you the fearlessness and you befriend all the animals around you.

I lived in the woods, completely unprotected among a multitude of wild animals. Not once was I attacked by any animal, not even an insect. Once you gain the mastery of this chakra, fear of death leaves you.

The devi is surrounded by Amrita and other forms of energy. There are sixteen devis in the chakra *sadhana*, as per *Shri Vidya*, the purest science of the goddess. They are: Kamakarshini, Buddhyakarshini, Ahamkarakarshini, Shabdakarshini, Sparshakarshini, Rupakarhsini, Rasakarshini, Gandhakarshini, Chittakarshini, Dharyakarshini, Smrityikarshini, Namakarshini, Bijakarshini, Atmakarshini, Amrtakarshini and Sarirakarshini.

All of the above names end with a certain suffix '*karshini*'. It's a Sanskrit word that means the power of restraint or more importantly the power of correct use, the wisdom of application. The above sixteen names refer to love, intelligence, self conceptualization, sound, touch, form, taste, smell, consciousness, valor, memory, identity, creative fluid, etheral body and physical body respectively. After meditating on the previous chakras and by the time you finish with this one, you become extremely mindful and diligent at all times, you exercise great vigilance in conducting yourself and you put to use the above sixteen elements in the rightmost, finest manner.

The devi's name is Dakini and the accompanying sound is DAM.

THE BROW PLEXUS

AGYA CHAKRA

Right on your glabella, between your brows, is the *agya* (or *ajna*) chakra, the brow plexus.

> *"ājñācakrābjanilayā śuklavarṇā ṣaḍānanā.*
> *majjāsaṃsthā haṃsavatīmukhyaśaktisamanvitā,*
> *haridrānnaikarasikā hākinīrūpadhāriṇī."*
> (*Lalita Sahasranama*, 107.5-108)

THE LITERAL MEANING

Situated in the *agya* chakra, the plexus between your brows, there is a six-faced devi of pure white color. Established in the bone marrow, she is attended by the primary energy called Hamsavati. She likes sumptuous foods cooked with a bit of turmeric and assumes the form of Hakini.

THE ESOTERIC MEANING

The devi is no longer holding any weapons, which means that there is nothing to battle now. The practitioner simply has to rise above the last set of challenges, which will happen effortlessly now. White is the color of peace and the devi is six-faced. The student now remains established in peace and the six faces of the devi represent six profound changes that every living creature goes through; she represents the six infirmities and the six inner foes. Before I expound on these, it is important to note that if you have been sincerely carrying out the meditation on the lower five chakras, if you have reached here in a devoted manner, step-by-step, none of the six aspects of changes, infirmities or foes can ever move you, lure you, distract you, deviate you. They will all simply merge in you. You will become bigger than them.

The six changes are birth, existence, growth, transformation, decay and disappearance. The six infirmities are hunger, thirst, grief, delusion, old age and death. The six foes are passion, anger, greed, attachment, pride and envy. Even for a yogi, these can be real challenges. They can cause fear. They can prompt the practitioner to engage in misconduct. Meditating on the *agya* chakra, however, germinates the seed of wisdom and stillness in you.

You start to see things in an entirely new perspective. It doesn't mean you no longer need to feed or clothe yourself. It simply means that you develop extraordinary patience and endurance. For starters, you maintain a constant awareness of the temporary nature of this world. You begin to realize that you have a greater role to play than simply feeding your own desires. This feeling unclutters your mind. Waves of bliss wash away negative emotions.

Selfless service takes the place of selfish desires. This new cleansing leaves you more satisfied and contented with much less.

Your desires diminish a great deal, as a result of which your needs come down automatically. You no longer need a lot of attention, wealth, fame or even love. The need to cling to someone or crave for their time starts to disappear. At this stage, you are rapidly moving towards the eternal fountain of bliss within you, your journey of turning inward is coming to a close. Mastering the *agya* chakra marks the beginning of the end.

As I have mentioned repeatedly, there are no shortcuts. If you can come this far with persistence, focus and dedication, you are a rare gem, one in ten million, if not one in a hundred million. The only thing you need to know is that if you get to this stage, nature will carve out a plan for you. It'll use you as an instrument to serve a higher purpose.

The devi of this chakra is situated in the bone marrow. Meditating on this chakra can help you get rid of any physical disorders in the bone marrow. It also signifies that meditation is now in your very bones. Earlier you had to try and meditate, but now it will just happen without trying. You are almost there, ready to discover your natural state of peace and bliss.

The attendant devi is called Hamsavati. It refers to one of the most profound practices one can do on the formless Divine. When you inhale you say '*hamsa*' and when you exhale you say '*soham*'. It means, 'I am that'. There is no greater realization than actually feeling, in every moment of your life, that you are the Divine you are seeking and that everything and everyone around you is just as divine.

When you reach this far in your *sadhana*, you no longer worry about the benefits because you don't weigh everything in terms of gain or loss. You've risen above such duality long ago by now.

While meditating on this chakra, consume delicious but healthy food and it's good to have a bit of turmeric in your savory food items. The name of the devi is Hakini and the syllable is HAM.

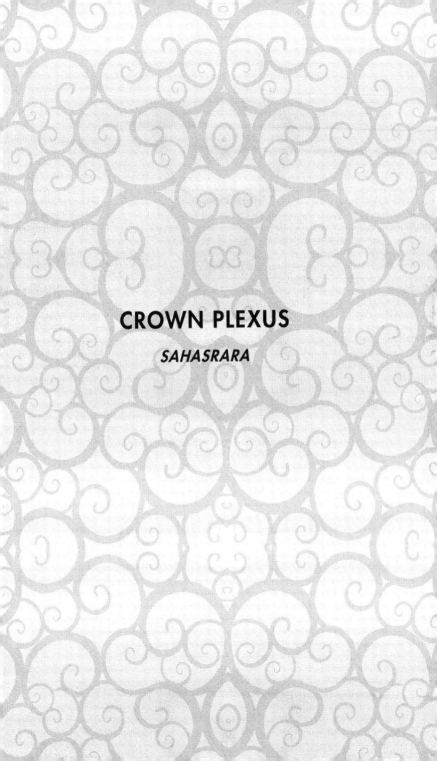

CROWN PLEXUS

SAHASRARA

A t the crown of your head, spreads the most beautiful lotus of a thousand petals, *sahasrara*.

> "*sahasradalapadmasthā sarvavarṇopaśobhitā,*
> *sarvāyudhadharā śuklasaṃsthitā sarvatomukhī.*
> *sarvaudanaprītacittā yākinyambāsvarūpiṇī.*"
> (*Lalita Sahasranama*, 109-110.5)

THE LITERAL MEANING

Situated in the thousand-petalled lotus, adorned with all the letters of the Sanskrit alphabet, holding all the implements, firmly established in the creative fluid, facing all the directions, all types of food is dear to her, she is known as Yakini.

THE ESOTERIC MEANING

The word *sahasra* means multifold, literally for one thousand. In *Lalita Sahasranama*, goddess is called the one with thousand faces, thousand eyes and thousand hands (*sahasraśīrṣa-vadanā sahasrākṣī sahasrapāt*). *Sahasrara* is your entry point to being that goddess. When you reach *sahasrara*, your existence and your abilities grow manifold.

Sahasrara is not really a chakra; it's a stage, a state, an outcome. It is your portal to infinite possibilities. You are no longer just one person struggling through life or trying to attain a goal. Instead, you become an embodiment of divinity, of the Goddess. The momentum, focus and power of your every thought grow in multiples of thousands. It's like you have thousands of hands to assist you.

Reaching *sahasrara* is the reward of your intense *sadhana*. A practitioner who has reached this stage has become an adept. The *sadhaka*, seeker, has gone beyond even being a *siddha*, an accomplished one. He has reached the ultimate level of being a *sadhya*, the one they sought. The seeker has gained union with the one he had been seeking.

At this level you are worthy of adoration because your existence is completely selfless and for the welfare of others. You gain the power – to heal people, to do miracles, to see through them. Boundless compassion comes to you naturally and you attract people like a flower attracts honeybees.

The word thousand in this verse is meant to signify not strictly one thousand but a large number. It was common in the ancient texts to refer to 'a lot' as *shata* (literal for one hundred) and 'more than a lot' as *sahasara*. By thousand-petalled lotus, it is meant that you have gone beyond the lotuses and their petals, they are in abundance now. You are a giant ocean of such lotuses at this stage.

All the letters of the alphabet reside in this chakra. Anything we speak or write is constructed using letters of the alphabet. It's not about any literal placement of such letters. Instead, it signifies that you have reached a stage where there is nothing left for you to seek anymore. You gain a remarkable insight into the reality of all the things. You gain the ultimate power of truth, understanding and compassion.

The one at this stage has gone beyond the physical elements of blood, bones, fat, marrow etc. You now reside in the creative fluid, you are the creative fluid. The creative fluid does not refer to semen alone. It refers to *ojas* in Ayurveda, an aspect both men and women possess. No more one, two, three or four faces, instead you see in all the directions. You have become an emperor or empress of your own world. You write your own destiny at this level.

Your resolutions, your thoughts – they manifest for you. Your wish is Nature's command. Anything you seriously aim for will come to fruition. Everything you taste feels amazing, you have risen above the rules; you are free to do, eat, be and wear whatever you want, for you have gained independence from the clutches of your own mind. Profound physical sensations of bliss overtake you completely.

After my vision of Mother Divine, I started experiencing deep sensations, powerful sensations in my brain. It was as if someone was kneading dough inside my brain, especially in my forehead and then extending to the whole brain. The sensations would start from the palate of the mouth. There was no pain but there was a feeling of extraordinary pressure.

In the beginning when I used to put my head down for resting, the sensations would build up and my head used to hurt. There was no pain inside my brain, just tremendous force, it was as if someone was putting pressure on my brain and with ever present concentrative state, such sensations would continue to build up. It took me a while to learn to live with them. Initially, I'd thought that they would go away but they never did. They are just as powerful today as they were originally.

Just like the Ganges emerges from Gangotri drop by drop and becomes a wide, full and meandering river merging all the way in Gangasagar, the nectar drips from *sahasrara* drop by drop and travels through my whole being filling me with bliss.

The devi is known by the name of Yakini. The syllable is YAM. The root letter '*Ya*' means This. This is it, Now.

This is the primary difference between an adept and an aspirer; an adept rejoices where a seeker struggles. The accomplished one lives from where the student runs and that is, Now.

A FINAL WORD

The path of *advaita*, non-duality, in the Vedas says that God is formless and that 'I am That'. There is no difference between *atma* (soul) and *paramatma* (supreme soul). Hence, both are equal, and everyone is God. Bhakti, on the other hand, says that you are not merely an *atma* but *jivatma*, an embodied soul, who is polluted. Bhakti says that you are full of selfish desires and emotions. It suggests that you have committed many sins whereas God is sinless. Therefore, no merger is possible between the ever-pure supreme soul and the eternally impure embodied soul.

Bhakti says ask for forgiveness of your sins and surrender yourself completely to the Divine will by chanting his holy names and singing his glories.

Tantra disagrees.

The fundamental difference between Vedic and tantric thought is your take on God. In tantra you say, "You are my object of worship. You are superior than I am and that is why I'm praying to you. But, I'm not merely interested in eulogizing or seeking pardon for my sins. I want to purify myself to the extent where I merge in you and you merge in me, so that one day I become you. I'm not interested in this union after I die; I want to experience it while I live.

> "*Yairēva patanaṁ dravyaiḥ sid'dhistairava cōditā,*
> *Śrīkauladarśanē caiva bhairavēṇa mahātmanā.*"
> (*Kularnava Tantra*, 5, 48)
>
> **The Great Bhairava (Shiva) of the *Kaula* tradition has instructed that spiritual advancement can only be attained by utilizing the very things that cause a man's downfall.**

Kundalini is my energy after all, so are my emotions and thoughts. Tantra says nothing is good or bad on its own. It all depends on its application or utilization. The path of kundalini *sadhana* admits that I have shortcomings and flaws. But, I can't let them destroy my self-worth. Tantra emphasizes that to rise above anything you have to understand it.

When you don't understand something you suppress it, you deny it, and such denial is your greatest obstruction on the path of awakening. Instead, transform all your negativity and limitations into a potent force that's focused on attainment of liberation.

Tantra recommends that you let everything be at ease so you may examine it, understand it, tame it and transcend it. You should feel bad thinking that you are full of sins. Instead, walk through your sins and go to their root. Someone has to clean the garbage. Ignoring it is not cleaning it. It'll only sit there and stink. You have to learn to handle everything that exists in you, skillfully, artfully.

A jungle can't only have all lions or deer. It will have hyneas and elephants too. It'll be a home to birds and insects as well. You can't only have all good emotions in one person. I'm a mix but let me use this mix to colour the canvas of my existence. If the primal force is kundalini, the purest essence, the goddess, then all one has to do is use one's energies to strip oneself off the conditioning so you may unveil your own potential. If God is in everything, then can anything in his existence be unwholesome? This is the path of tantra.

Awakening of kundalini is a tantric *sadhana*.

A caterpillar is not born with wings but among its struggles in the cocoon, in an effort to come out of its shell, it continues to meditate, it dreams of flying. From a spineless grub, an unsightly larva, it turns into a pupa hanging upside down from the branch of some tree. It can hang there from a few days to several weeks and months.

A worm like caterpillar can't possibly fly. It has no wings, but it has hope, it has faith. It is as if the larva has understood that if it wants to fly, it has to transform itself into a creature far different from what it is presently. It must become lighter. It must persist with its metamorphosis.

Patiently, the pupa meditates on a butterfly. Quietly, it

continues to shed its layers. Gradually, it starts to notice a change in itself. The new layers are harder, it doesn't feel like a worm anymore, tiny parts are protruding on its back that may well be the wings. It continues with faith on the path of transformation. And one day, the shell opens just enough to let the pupa out. It drops itself out of the cocoon. And the unthinkable happens. Rather than falling flat on the ground, its wings spread themselves and it takes a flight.

It is no longer a caterpillar spitting strands of silk or a pupa hanging upside down. It becomes a beautiful butterfly with wings and colours. Its life takes a new dimension. Out of the confines of a dark cocoon, it now flits about on fragrant flowers in green gardens, in daylight, in beauty. It gains new abilities even though it has no supporting organs. A butterfly is able to smell without a nose, for example. This extraordinary metamorphosis from caterpillar to butterfly is the path of kundalini awakening, it is the essence of all tantric *sadhana*.

How long it takes depends on the quality of your moral, mental and physical discipline. How long a larva hangs upside down depends on its type. Some are done in days while it takes months for others before they are able to step out of the cocoon. The more resolute you are to shed your layers and the more disciplined is your effort, the faster will be your transformation.

In *Lalita Sahasranama*, immediately after the exposition on the chakras, it says:

> *"svāhā svadhā'matir medhā śrutiḥ smṛtir anuttamā.*
> *puṇyakīrtiḥ puṇyalabhyā puṇyaśravaṇakīrtanā,*
> *pulomajārcitā bandhamocanī barbarālakā."*
> (*Lalita Sahasranama*, 110.5 –111)

These verses are not thereby accident but by careful design. In their literal meaning, these lines merely list the different names of the Goddess. It means that the Goddess is the one who takes oblations to the gods and ablutions to the ancestors. She is the foremost thought, intelligence, worth listening to, memory. She brings merit, fame and gain to the devotees, who sing her glories. Worshipped by even the greatest like Puloma (wife of the great sage Bhrigu), she severs all bonds and is supremely enchanting.

In reality though, its esoteric meaning conveys the spiritual progress of a seeker. The first word *svaha* implies that you have completely burnt all your proclivities, your negative tendencies. Like the caterpillar, you burn your disbelief that you can't grow wings. You no longer focus on what you can't do, instead you simply meditate on what you wish to do and let the Universe conspire to make it happen for you.

The next word *svadha* also means innate power and the inherent ability to absorb. At the awakening of the kundalini, you realize your extraordinary talents, the immense potential that you always had in you. Like the pupa you continue to shed your layers of inhibitions and fears. With each layer you molt, you discover a new aspect of you. You sense that you can grow wings after all, you figure that must step out of the cocoon.

Subsequent words (*matir medhā śrutiḥ smṛtir anuttamā*) mean that on the path of awakening, the quality and force of your thought and intelligence gains tremendous momentum as you unlock secrets of existence unknown to the mankind. The scattered mind becomes a focused beam. Your memory becomes sharp and you are able to store and recall vast amounts of information. You are second to none. You realize that you can be whatever or whoever you want to be, that your job is to not be tied by a million strands, even if of silk, but to taste the nectar from all the flowers you so wish.

The remaining words in the verse mean that you become a rare gem in the universe. With your mere presence, mere thought, people around you will experience bliss and liberation. Nature then chooses you to do the major work and fame and glory of your meritorious acts and wisdom spread far and wide. Every word uttered by you benefits the mankind in one way or another. Even the brightest minds will seek refuge in you and will experience freedom, peace and joy.

That's how sages of the yore, like Ved Vyasa, Agastya and many others attained unimaginable spiritual heights. That's why even in a religion like Buddhism, which denies the existence of both soul and the supreme soul, there is extensive literature on kundalini and chakras. Even Buddha, the Gautama, attained enlightenment at the awakening of kundalini, as the Buddhist scriptures tell. Buddha himself might not have called it kundalini, but his realization of virginal awareness and subsequent introduction of chakras point to the truth of this primordial energy.

Like a caterpillar breaks free of the cocoon and flies off a butterfly, at the awakening of kundalini, you break free of your conditioning. A new 'you' is unveiled from underneath. Layers of anger, hatred, jealousy, selfishness, attachments and ego are removed at the piercing of each chakra, and you become a living reflection, an embodiment, of Devi herself. This transformation brings about an inexplicable feeling of oneness with the cosmic energy, a tremendous feeling of fearlessness.

If you feel that this sounds too good to be true, I don't blame you. There was a time when I too had my doubts regarding the truth of kundalini. It all sounded a bit too unreal. Was it possible to experience that deep bliss in this day and age? Could kundalini actually lead to a complete union with the divine energy? Would its awakening really leave one completely fearless? During or after my intense *sadhana*, I didn't levitate, fly in the air or reduce my body to the size of an atom. But, prolonged meditation with deep concentration did produce remarkable vibrations and sensations in my whole body. Contrary to the popular (mis)belief, these weren't the shaking of the body or seeing the blinding light. Instead, these were the powerful sensations that began to gather up in my forehead and then in the crown of my head.

I thought if my constant deep sensations were a sure sign of the awakening of kundalini then I ought to test it. I needed to know if I had actually become the Goddess myself, if the primordial energy had manifested herself in me.

I remember I would step out in the middle of the night in the Himalayan woods to be among the wild animals, to test if I still had any fears in me, for the fear of death ultimately triumphs all other fears. I would sit in areas infested by snakes and scorpions. In the middle of the night, I would go offer oblations in the river where feline cats, being nocturnal, were more likely to greet me. I would walk up to viciously barking wild dogs and they would quieten. They would wag their tail and sit right there. They would roll on the ground.

I would not be telling you the complete truth if I were to say that I simply went out to test if I had conquered the fear of death. The truth is: I also wanted to see if they too felt the Goddess in me. I needed to know if we were truly connected with each other through the same primordial energy. I wanted to see if they, the wild and untamed ones, could feel the same love for me as I had felt for them.

I realized one thing more clearly than ever before: there lies the same life force beneath various shapes, species and behavior of all living entities. I call her Devi, the Goddess. Below the fears of sentient beings flows the river of love and compassion. It is the reason that over and over again we fall in love, seek love, give love, because that's who we are, beings of love. We are naturally attracted to what we are made of – love.

With awakening comes the realization that love is the only emotion worth harboring and spreading. You become an embodiment of selfless love for that is what kundalini is. Kundalini is love coiled at the bottom of your desires and dreams, waiting to pierce through the wheels of emotions and attachments to attain a union with your own infinite existence. It is the realization that you are not an isolated drop of water, which will dry up any moment, but an integral part of an eternal water body – an ocean. Oceans never dry up.

Earth never loses its solidity. Wind and light never turn old. Fire never stops burning. Water never stops flowing; it may freeze, it may evaporate but it turns back into water. Your fears may shape you. They may freeze you or dissipate you, but eventually you return to your original state.

Lines and wrinkles might appear on your face, your body might age, your vitality might diminish, but the primal energy in you, the kundalini, remains eternally youthful. She is passionate and sportive, beyond all decay and death. Allow Shakti to unite with Shiva, let your energy meet with your potential so you may see the immensity of the one who lives in you, so you may see how complete, youthful and beautiful you are. This realization and discovery will baffle you. It'll surprise you and it'll transform you forever.

This is my experience of awakening. Go, find yours.

GLOSSARY

Adharma is the opposite of dharma. That which is not in accord with the dharma. Connotations include unnaturalness, wrongness, evil, immorality, wickedness, and vice.

Adityas are solar deities residing in the celestial regions. They represent various cosmic phenomena that help in the sustenance of the Universe. The twelve adityas are Varuna, Mitra, Aryama, Bhaga, Amshuman, Dhata, Indra, Savitur, Tvashtha, Vishnu, Pushya, Vivasvan. Vishnu is the chief of all adityas.

Aghoris are ascetics who engage in extreme austerities, often taboo, to experience oneness with Shiva.

Amavasya is the night of the new moon.

Brahma Granthi means the knot of Brahma. This is covered in detail in the fourth chapter titled The Three Knots.

Brahmarishi is a member of the highest class of seers.

Dakshinayana is the period when the sun travels from Cancer to Sagittarius. This southward journey of the sun from summer to winter solstice consists of three seasons: rainy season, autumn, and most of winter.

Damaru is a small two-headed drum used by Lord Shiva.

Dandavata pranama is the most reverential form of greeting in the Vedic tradition. It means full-length prostration.

Darshana is auspicious sight of a holy person, which bestows merit. It also means a system of philosophy, but here it specifically means a holy vision.

Devaloka is the abode of gods.

Devas are celestial beings or gods.

Devi bhava refers to being in the devotional sentiment of Goddess. When a devotee's consciousness is yoked to Devi, he or she performs every action with utmost divinity.

Dhyana refers to a state of deep meditation or contemplation. In Patanjali's yoga sutras, it is the stage before Samadhi which means profound absorption or a state of perfect insight and tranquillity.

Ganas mean body of attendants or a flock.

Gandharvas are celestial musicians.

Har Har Mahadev is a form of slogan or salutation meaning all glories to Lord Shiva

Indra is the ruler of all gods, below the holy trinity of Brahma, Vishnu and Shiva. In the Hindu tradition, he is also the god of rains.

Indraloka is the abode of Indra.

Jai Bajrang Bali means Hail Lord Bajrang Bali, another name of Hanumana.

Kevala nirvikalpa samadhi is the ultimate form of samadhi in yoga. Nirvikalpa samadhi literally means a samadhi without any other alternative. It means that mental activity (citta vritti) has come to a complete cessation and there's no distinction between the knower, the act of knowing and the object of knowledge. It's a complete union like drops of water merging in the ocean. Kevala nirvikalpa samadhi means the practitioner has been absorbed in this samadhi for very long period already.

Kusha is a type of grass used in almost all Hindu religious ceremonies. In the olden days, sleeping and meditation mats were made from stalks of kusha grass.

Namoh Parvati Pataye is generally used as a slogan meaning Salutations to Lord Shiva, the consort of Parvati.

Pativrata means a virtuous wife. Particularly the one who has never eyed any man other than her husband, let alone being intimate with one.

Prajapati means lord of people presiding over procreation and protection of life.

Purushottama refers to the supreme being, the finest among all men.

Rishi means an ascetic, sage or seer.

Ritwik means the chief priest.

Rudra Granthi is the knot of Shiva. It is covered in detail in the fourth chapter titled The Three Knots.

Sadhaka is someone who does sadhana. An aspirant or practitioner committed to a set of spiritual practices is a sadhaka.

Sadhana is a spiritual practice or a set of spiritual practices leading to self-realization.

Sahasrara is the crown chakra. It is generally considered the seventh primary chakra.

Samadhi is the final stage of meditation. It means deep tranquil absorption or a complete union with the divinity within and without.

Samhita refers to the most ancient forms of texts, often composed by seers, in the Vedas consisting of mantras, hymns, prayers, litanies and benedictions.

Siddha is an adept.

Stotra means an ode, eulogy or a hymn of praise.

Tapasvin means a practitioner of austerities, an ascetic.

Tapasya means austerity, spiritual practise or penance.

Uttarayana is the period when the sun travels from Capricorn to Cancer, i.e. from south to north. This northward journey of the sun from winter to summer solstice consists of three seasons: the end of winter, spring and summer.

Vanara means a monkey or an ape.

Vastu is an ancient system of architecture. Its literal translation is the science of architecture.

Vasus are attendant deities of Indra and later Vishnu.

Vidya means a school of thought or a form of worship. In the science of mantras, the sacred syllables belonging to invoking the feminine energy is also called vidya. Correct knowledge or a certain skill is also known as vidya.

Vishnu Granthi refers to the knot of Vishnu. This is covered in detail in the fourth chapter titled The Three Knots.

Yajna refers to ritual sacrifice with a specific objective in mind or fire offerings for the welfare of all sentient beings.

Yuga means an epoch or era within a four age cycle. One cycle of four yugas represents an arc and spans 25,92,000 years. The four yugas are satya (1,728,000 years), treta (1,296,000 years), dwapra (864,000 years) and kali (432,000 years). According to the Hindu tradition, the current yuga is the age of kali.

Made in the USA
San Bernardino, CA
31 July 2019